SIDNEY WARREN, the editor of this book, is Professor of Political Science and History at California Western University in San Diego. Among his authoritative studies of the Presidency are *The President as a World Leader,* the forthcoming *Battle for the Presidency,* and numerous articles for *Current History,* the *Saturday Review,* and other magazines and journals.

THE AMERICAN PRESIDENT

edited by

Sidney Warren

PRENTICE-HALL, INC. *Englewood Cliffs, New Jersey*

To RUTH *and* DAVID

PREFACE

WITHIN THE LIFETIME of one generation, the United States has soared to a preeminent position among the nations of the world, its capital the center of leadership for a vast agglomeration of states. Its power and responsibilities could not have been imagined by the architects of the Republic in their most extravagant dreams for its future. Concomitantly, the President's role has become uniquely significant—the welfare of 200 million citizens at home and the destiny of many more millions around the globe are vitally affected by the policies and decisions that emanate from the White House.

This book of readings is designed to provide for both the student and the layman a deeper understanding of the dimension, the complexity, and the subtleties of Presidential leadership. For background, the first section deals with the place of the Presidency in the Constitution and how it has evolved over the years. Inasmuch as the views of the Chief Executive color and determine the nature of his leadership, the next section contains examples of how the office has been regarded by some of the men who have occupied it. In the third section, leading commentators view the office from the outside looking in. And in the final section, the Presidency is examined by means of official statements and policies that reflect the wide-ranging roles that both constitutional duty and historical circumstance have required the Chief Executive to perform.

Through these four categories, I believe a clear picture emerges of the multifaceted and highly complex nature of what is now the most important office in the world.

S.W.

CONTENTS

ix

part three

████████████████

THE AMERICAN PRESIDENT

part one

░░░░░░░░░░░░░░

A NEW DEPARTURE

Between the time the Declaration of Independence was proclaimed and the Constitution of the United States was adopted, eleven years elapsed. During that period the Continental Congress established a confederation which bound thirteen separate entities into a national governmental structure. At the same time, new state governments were created. With vivid memories of colonial assemblies chafing under the arbitrary use of power by the royal governors, these new governments provided that weak executives would be checked and restrained by legislative bodies. This mistrust of a strong chief executive also accounts for the omission from the Articles of Confederation of a separate and independent executive branch.

For a number of reasons, it was soon apparent that the existing confederation of states was not viable. A more enduring instrument of government was required to replace it. This need presented both an opportunity and a challenge. While these architects of statecraft agreed that a stronger central government was imperative, they could not agree to its precise form. Schooled in political philosophy but well steeped in practical politics, they debated how authority should be distributed, how representation apportioned and how power restrained; they did not debate in abstract terms, but in the practical context of best promoting and protecting geographical sections and economic classes, and of reconciling the national interests to the local. Statesmen as well as politicians, they compromised their differences for the sake of achieving a common goal.

One of the major constitutional debates concerned the form of the executive branch. Monarchy was rejected as well as cabinet government, with its fusion of executive and legislative departments. Turning away from the familiar, they settled upon an executive branch of government which was to be headed by a President. Experience had mitigated their distrust of a strong executive. The Founding Fathers brought imagination to the art of statecraft, and made a significant departure from the past, when they designed the Presidency.

I

James Madison to Thomas Jefferson

The nature and design of the Presidency was at the very heart of the problems of a new governmental structure with which the delegates to the Constitutional Convention had to grapple. Working long and tirelessly, they considered various alternatives. In a letter to Thomas Jefferson, James Madison summarized the conflicting views aired in the convention, and indicated his own position. He referred particularly to problems posed by the Presidency—the manner of election, the tenure in office, the chief executive's independence and duties. The Madisonian concept, which emphasized checks and balances to restrain presidential authority, was later to compete with the Hamiltonian approach, which relied upon extra-constitutional devices to strengthen executive power.

New York, Octr 24, 1787

YOU WILL HEREWITH receive the result of the Convention, which continued its session till the 17th of September. I take the liberty of making some observations on the subject, which will help to make up a letter, if they should answer no other purpose.

It appeared to be the sincere and unanimous wish of the Convention to cherish and preserve the Union of the States. No proposition was made, no suggestion was thrown out, in favor of a partition of the Empire into two or more Confederacies.

It was generally agreed that the objects of the Union could not be secured by any system founded on the principle of a confederation of Sovereign States. A *voluntary* observance of the federal law by all the members could never be hoped for. A *compulsive* one could evidently never be reduced to practice, and if it could, involved equal calamities to the innocent and the guilty, the necessity of a military force both obnoxious and dangerous, and in general a scene resembling much more a civil war than the administration of a regular Government.

Hence was embraced the alternative of a Government which instead of operating, on the States, should operate without their intervention on

Max Farrand, The Records of the Federal Convention of 1787 *(New Haven, Conn.: Yale University Press, 1937), III, 132-133. Copyright 1911, 1937 by Yale University Press. Reprinted by permission.*

the individuals composing them; and hence the change in the principle and proportion of representation.

This ground-work being laid, the great objects which presented themselves were 1. to unite a proper energy in the Executive, and a proper stability in the Legislative departments, with the essential characters of Republican Government. 2. to draw a line of demarcation which would give to the General Government every power requisite for general purposes, and leave to the States every power which might be most beneficially administered by them. 3. to provide for the different interests of different parts of the Union. 4. to adjust the clashing pretensions of the large and small States. Each of these objects was pregnant with difficulties. The whole of them together formed a task more difficult than can be well conceived by those who were not concerned in the execution of it. Adding to these considerations the natural diversity of human opinions on all new and complicated subjects, it is impossible to consider the degree of concord which ultimately prevailed as less than a miracle.

The first of these objects, as respects the Executive, was peculiarly embarrassing. On the question whether it should consist of a single person, or a plurality of co-ordinate members, on the mode of appointment, on the duration in office, on the degree of power, on the reeligibility, tedious and reiterated discussions took place. The plurality of co-ordinate members had finally but few advocates. Governour Randolph was at the head of them. The modes of appointment proposed were various, as by the people at large—by electors chosen by the people—by the Executives of the States—by the Congress, some preferring a joint ballot of the two Houses—some a separate concurrent ballot, allowing to each a negative on the other house—some, a nomination of several candidates by one House, out of whom a choice should be made by the other. Several other modifications were started. The expedient at length adopted seemed to give pretty general satisfaction to the members. As to the duration in office, a few would have preferred a tenure during good behaviour—a considerable number would have done so in case an easy and effectual removal by impeachment could be settled. It was much agitated whether a long term, seven years for example, with a subsequent and perpetual ineligibility, or a short term with a capacity to be re-elected, should be fixed. In favor of the first opinion were urged the danger of a gradual degeneracy of re-elections from time to time, into first a life and then a hereditary tenure, and the favorable effect of an incapacity to be reappointed on the independent exercise of the Executive authority. On the other side it was contended that the prospect of necessary degradation would discourage the most dignified characters from aspiring to the office, would take away the principal motive to ye faithful discharge of its duties—the hope of being rewarded with a re-appointment would stimulate ambition to violent efforts for holding over the constitutional term—and instead of producing an independent administration, and a firmer defence of the constitutional rights of the department, would render the officer more indifferent to the importance of a place which he would soon be obliged to quit forever, and more ready to yield to the encroachments of the Legislature of which he might again be a member. The questions concerning the degree of power turned chiefly on the appointment to offices, and the control on the Legislature. An *absolute* appointment to all offices—to some offices—to no offices, formed the scale of opinions on the first point. On the second, some contended for an absolute negative, as the only possible means of reducing to practice the theory of a free Government which forbids a mixture of the Legislative and Executive powers. Others would be content with a revisionary power, to be overruled by three fourths of both Houses. It was warmly urged that the judiciary department should be associated in the revision. The idea of some was that a separate revision should be given to the two departments—that if either objected two thirds, if both, three fourths, should be necessary to overrule. . .

2

Alexander Hamilton on the Presidency

In the discussions which led to the creation of the office of the President, competing arguments were advanced by those who saw merit both in a single and a plural composition of the executive. Hamilton strongly advocated the former, asserting that public opinion could more exactly assess responsibility for policy if the executive were single. He saw another advantage that would help to safeguard the nation's security, an advantage which neither a plural executive nor a legislative body possessed: the faculty of acting with speed and in secrecy. The presidential system which Hamilton supported, and which was finally adopted by the Constitutional Convention, had no precedent.

Alexander Hamilton, Federalist, *No. 70.*

THERE IS AN idea, which is not without its advocates, that a vigorous Executive is inconsistent with the genius of republican government. The enlightened well-wishers to this species of government must at least hope that the supposition is destitute of foundation; since they can never admit its truth, without, at the same time, admitting the condemnation of their own principles. Energy in the Executive is a leading character in the definition of good government. It is essential to the protection of the community against foreign attacks; it is not less essential to the steady administration of the laws, to the protection of property against those irregular and high-handed combinations, which sometimes interrupt the ordinary course of justice, to the security of liberty against the enterprises and assaults of ambition, of faction, and of anarchy. Every man, the least conversant in Roman story, knows how often that republic was obliged to take refuge in the absolute power of a single man, under the formidable title of dictator, as well as against the intrigues of ambitious individuals, who aspired to the tyranny, and the seditions of whole classes of the community, whose conduct threatened the existence of all government, as against the invasions of external enemies, who menaced the conquest and destruction of Rome.

There can be no need, however, to multiply arguments or examples on this head. A feeble Executive implies a feeble execution of the government. A feeble execution is but another phrase for a bad execution; and a government ill executed, whatever it may be in theory, must be, in practice, a bad government.

Taking it for granted, therefore, that all men of sense will agree in the necessity of an energetic Executive, it will only remain to inquire, what are the ingredients which constitute this energy? How far can they be combined with those other ingredients, which constitute safety in the republican sense? And how far does this combination characterize the plan which has been reported by the convention?

The ingredients which constitute energy in the Executive are, unity; duration; an adequate provision for its support; competent powers.

The ingredients which constitute safety in the republican sense are, a due dependence on the people; a due responsibility.

Those politicians and statesmen, who have been the most celebrated for the soundness of their principles, and for the justness of their views, have declared in favor of a single Executive, and a numerous legislature. They have, with great propriety, considered energy as the most necessary qualification of the former, and have regarded this as most applicable to power in a single hand; while they have, with equal propriety, considered the latter as best adapted to deliberation and wisdom, and best calculated to conciliate the confidence of the people, and to secure their privileges and interests.

That unity is conducive to energy will not be disputed. Decision, activity, secrecy, and dispatch, will generally characterize the proceedings of one man, in a much more eminent degree than the proceedings of any greater number; and in proportion as the number is increased, these qualities will be diminished.

This unity may be destroyed in two ways; either by vesting the power in two or more magistrates, of equal dignity and authority; or by vesting it ostensibly in one man, subject, in whole or in part, to the control and co-operation of others, in the capacity of counsellors to him. . . .

The experience of other nations will afford little instruction on this head. As far, however, as it teaches anything, it teaches us not to be enamoured of plurality in the Executive. . . .

Wherever two or more persons are engaged in any common enterprise or pursuit, there is always danger of difference of opinion. If it be a public trust of office, in which they are clothed with equal dignity and authority, there is peculiar danger of personal emulation and even animosity. From either, and especially from all these causes, the most bitter dissentions are apt to spring. Whenever these happen, they lessen the respectability, weaken the authority, and distract the plans and operations of those whom they divide. If they should unfortunately assail the supreme executive magistracy of a country, consisting of a plurality of persons, they might impede or frustrate the most important measures of the government, in the most critical emergencies of the state. And what is still worse, they might split the community into violent and irreconcilable factions, adhering differently to the different individuals who composed the magistracy. . . .

Upon the principles of a free government, inconveniences from the source just mentioned, must necessarily be submitted to in the formation of the legislature; but it is unnecessary, and therefore unwise, to introduce them into the constitution of the Executive. It is here, too, that they may be most pernicious. In the legislature, promptitude of decision is oftener an evil than a benefit. The differences of opinion, and the jarrings of parties in that department of the government, though they may sometimes obstruct salutary plans, yet often promote deliberation and circumspection; and serve to check excesses in the majority. When a resolution, too, is once taken, the opposition must be at an end. That resolution is a law, and resistance to it punishable. But no favorable circumstances palliate, or atone for the disadvantages of dissention in the executive department. Here they are pure and unmixed. There is no point at which they cease to operate. They serve to embarrass and weaken the execution of the plan or measure to which they relate, from the first step to the final conclusion of it. They constantly counteract those qualities in the Executive, which are the most necessary ingredients in its composition—vigor and expedition; and this without any counterbalancing good. In the conduct of war, in which the energy of the Executive is the bulwark of the national security, everything would have to be apprehended from its plurality.

It must be confessed, that these observations apply with principal weight to the first case supposed, that is, to a plurality of magistrates of equal dignity and authority, a scheme, the advocates for which are not likely to form a numerous sect; but they apply, though not with equal, yet with considerable weight, to the project of a council, whose concurrence is made constitutionally necessary to the operations of the ostensible executive. An artful cabal in that council would be able to distract and to enervate the whole system of administration. If no such cabal should exist, the mere diversity of views and opinions would alone be sufficient to tincture the exercise of the executive authority with the spirit of habitual feebleness and dilatoriness.

But one of the weightiest objections to a plurality in the Executive, and which lies as much against the last as the first plan, is, that it tends to conceal faults, and destroy responsibility. . . . It often becomes impossible, amidst mutual accusations, to determine on whom the blame or the punishment of a pernicious measure . . . ought really to fall. It is shifted from one to another with so much dexterity, and under such plausible appearances, that the public opinion is left in suspense about the real author. . . .

A little consideration will satisfy us, that the species of security sought for in the multiplication of the Executive, is unattainable. Numbers must be so great as to render combination difficult; or they are rather a source of danger than of security. The united credit and influence of several individuals must be more formidable to liberty than the credit and influence of either of them separately. When power, therefore, is placed in the hands of so small a number of men, as to admit of their interests and views being easily combined in a common enterprise, by an artful leader, it becomes more liable to abuse, and more dangerous when abused, than if it be lodged in the hands of one man;

who, from the very circumstance of his being alone, will be more narrowly watched and more readily suspected, and who cannot unite so great a mass of influence as when he is associated with others. . . .

I will only add, that prior to the appearance of the Constitution, I rarely met with an intelligent man from any of the states, who did not admit as the result of experience, that the unity of the executive of this state was one of the best of the distinguishing features of our Constitution.

3

The President in the Constitution

SIDNEY WARREN

In settling upon a plan which embodied the principle of equal and coordinate status for the executive branch, the framers of the Constitution gave the new American government a distinctive character. Essentially representing a compromise, the Presidency, both as it is defined in the Constitution and as it has developed over the years, remains unique among the world's governmental systems.

THE GROUP OF men who assembled in convention at Philadelphia in 1787 to draw up a fundamental law that would unite thirteen disunited states had brought with them conflicting viewpoints. For almost five months they labored, much of the time in the sweltering summer heat, until the document which emerged as the Constitution of the United States was finally completed. James Wilson, one of the delegates, reflecting on it later, called the construction of the presidency "the most difficult part of this system."

It is not surprising that this should have been true. The delegates divided sharply on the vital question of executive power. Some, recalling the unhappy era when most of the colonies were ruled by a Royal Governor, as the King's personal representative, had had the authority to make appointments, assume military command, control expenditures, issue pardons, and share in the process of law making. Though in time

Sidney Warren, "The President in the Constitution," Current History (September, 1953), pp. 133-137. Reprinted by permission.

the assemblies succeeded in undermining his authoritarian rule through control of supplies, friction never ceased.

More irritating than his coercive powers was the symbol he represented. His office was the point of tangency with the crown, and thus all the resentment against imperial control was inevitably directed against him.

During the Revolutionary War most of the state governments that were created reduced the office of governor almost to impotency. He was elected annually by the legislature and, unlike his colonial predecessor, lacked the power to summon, prorogue, or dissolve the assembly.

Only one governor was given the veto power, and it was taken away from him two years later. Even his purely executive functions had to be exercised in conjunction with a council of state chosen by the legislature.

There were some exceptions. The Pennsylvania constitution of 1776, for instance, bestowed all power not otherwise specifically provided for either to "the legislative or the executive according to its nature." The New York state constitution of 1777 provided for a governor to be elected by the people every three years without any limit to his re-eligibility. Except in the matter of appointments and vetoes he was not required to consult a council; he bore the title "Commander-in-Chief;" and he was charged with the duty of "taking care that the laws are faithfully executed to the best of his ability."

(It is interesting that the leading delegates to the Constitutional Convention from these two states were instrumental in shaping the office of president, and the phrasing of the New York constitution is strongly suggestive of the language later employed in Article II of the Federal Constitution.)

The prevailing feeling at the time the thirteen states banded together into a confederation was against executive domination. In the central government, the office of executive was conspicuous by its absence. A Congress conducted legislative affairs, made diplomatic and other appointments and handled treaties and other foreign relations, and the administration of government was carried on by committees which it appointed. The Whig doctrine of parliamentary supremacy was carried to a triumphant conclusion.

But the absence of an executive department, far from proving a blessing, turned out to be one of the major weaknesses of the new government. With members of congress paid by their respective states and serving mainly as delegates or ambassadors and responsible solely to their states, only an executive could have given the national leadership and unified command so urgently required.

With the limited central authority that did exist rendered nugatory by thirteen proud and unyielding separate sovereignties, the affairs of Government could not be carried on effectively. It is unnecessary to recount here the events leading to the decision to revise the Articles of Confederation and finally to abandon them in favor of an entirely new document. The men responsible for this action were determined to fashion a governmental structure that would survive periodic crises and vicissitudes.

CONSTITUTION FRAMERS

The lawmakers, Lord Bryce observed a century later, "included nearly all the best intellect and the ripest political experience that the United States then contained." Outstanding in that galaxy of brilliant minds, and those who had most to do with creating what was to be termed the Constitution of the United States, were the Scotsman James Wilson of Pennsylvania, student, lawyer, writer, who believed that all power should reside in the people; Gouverneur Morris, dandy and wit, who addressed the chair more than any other delegate; the aristocratic planter-lawyer-politician from South Carolina, Charles Pinckney; the precocious genius, Alexander Hamilton; Roger Sherman, who had been among other things surveyor, lawyer, merchant, and delegate to the Continental Congress for seven years; Edmond Randolph, "Virginia's able, unstable Governor"; and James Madison, brilliant parliamentary debator of encyclopedic reading and prodigious memory.

Eminently practical men, their ideas were shaped not only by their experiences but also by their familiarity with the works of such political theorists as Aristotle, Blackstone, Bolingbroke, Locke, and Montesquieu. To the last two, especially, they were intellectually indebted.

Both writers had advocated what might be termed a "balanced constitution," that is, initiation of legislation by both executive and legislative branches and the exercise by the executive of broad, discretionary, residual powers. Locke stated in his *Two Treatises of Government:*

Where the legislative and executive power are in distinct hands, as they are in all moderated monarchies and well-framed governments, there the good of the society requires that several things should be left to the discretion of him that has the executive power. For the legislators not being able to foresee and provide by laws for all that may be useful to the community, the executor of the laws, having the power in his hands, has by the common law of Nature a right to make use of it for the good of the society, in many cases where the municipal law has given no direction, till the legislative can conveniently be assembled to provide for it; nay, many things there are which the law can by no means provide for, and those must necessarily be left to the discretion of him that has the executive power in his hands, to be ordered by him as the public good and advantage shall require; nay, it is fit that the laws themselves should in some cases give way to the executive power, or rather to this fundamental law of Nature and government . . . that as much as may be all the members of the society are to be preserved.

And Montesquieu's espousal in explicit terms of government by separated and distinct departments provided the essence of the theory of a balanced constitution. As he said in his *Spirit of the Laws:*

When the legislative and executive powers are united in the same person, or in the same body of magistrates, there can be no liberty; because apprehensions may arise, lest the same monarch or senate should enact tyrannical laws, and execute them in a tyrannical manner.

With experience and theory to guide them, the delegates decided to place all political authority in the people and to establish a government containing three coordinate departments. The thorny question, now, was the nature of the executive for a government of this kind. What should be its form, powers, tenure, method of election and removal, and its relation to the other departments of the government?

It was essential to have executive power that would be capable of extending to the remotest parts of the Union in the event of serious emergencies. At the same time, care would have to be taken not to arouse the popular fear of monarchy.

The first problem that engaged the delegates was whether the office should be unitary or plural. Roger Sherman of Connecticut regarded the executive as little more than an institution to carry out the will of the legislature. He urged that the "number might not be fixed, but that the legislature should be at liberty to appoint one or more as experience might dictate." Both the Virginia and New Jersey plans supported him in recommending a plural executive. Madison felt that "A unity of the Executive would savor too much of a monarchy," and Butler feared that "It will terminate in a King."

Chief protagonist of the single executive was James Wilson, who advocated it "as giving most energy, dispatch and responsibility to the office." A plural system, he stated, would not produce tranquillity but "uncontrolled, continued and violent animosities." The Pinckney and Hamilton proposals also suggested a single executive. After considerable debate Wilson won his point, and the motion for a single executive was carried on June 4.

CHECK ON CONGRESS?

The major issue was yet to come: the relation of the executive to Congress. If his role was to be merely that of executing the laws of Congress, then the terms of his office, the method of his selection, the nature of his powers, and the provisions for his removal would naturally have to be different than if he were authorized to act as a check on legislative authority. In the one event, his dependence on Congress would make it mandatory for that body to be empowered to elect and remove him; in the other, he would have to be independent of it in those matters.

Here again the views of the delegates were widely divergent. James Wilson declared that "Any dependence of the executive on the Supreme Legislature is the very essence of tyranny." He urged his election by the people for a three-year term, with no limitation upon his re-eligibility.

Sherman insisted that the executive be elected by the legislative branch as a means of making him dependent upon it. Gouverneur Morris feared the dangers of legislative tyranny:

> One great object of the executive is to control the legislature. The legislature will continually seek to aggrandize and perpetuate themselves; and will seize those critical moments produced by invasion or convulsion for that purpose. It is necessary then that the Executive Magistrate should be the guardian of the people, even of the lower classes, against legislative tyranny, against the great and the wealthy who in the course of things will necessarily corrupt the legislative body. Wealth tends to corrupt the mind and nourish its love of power, and to stimulate it to oppression. . . . The Executive therefore ought to be so constituted as to be the great protector of the people.

To accomplish that objective, Morris saw no other way out than to have the executive elected by the people or to insure his appointment for life. The Virginia plan recommended election by the Congress of the executive with no re-eligibility, as did the New Jersey plan. Hamilton proposed indirect election of the executive by electors, without any limitation on re-eligibility.

At last the delegates rejected the method of popular choice as well as choice by electors and unanimously approved selection by the legislature. That was in July. On September 1 a new Committee of Eleven was set up to expedite "such parts of the Constitution as have been postponed." Three days later, reporting several proposals pertaining to the office of "the President," as it was now called, the Committee completely reversed the stand previously approved.

It recommended a four-year term for the president and vice-president and their selection by a body of electors appointed by each state equal to the number of senators and representatives from that state. The person who received the majority of the votes would be president, the second, vice-president. If no one received a majority, the names of the five having the highest number of votes would be submitted to the Senate, which would then select the two officers.

This precipitated the last of the great debates on the presidency. Gouverneur Morris, who was largely responsible for the Committee's action, defended it for going contrary to sentiment clearly expressed by the delegates weeks earlier.

He gave a number of reasons against election of the executive by the legislature: "Danger of intrigue and faction" controlling the outcome; ineligibility for re-election was undesirable but would be a necessary stipulation to avert recurring factional politics over the re-election issue; in the event of impeachment proceedings a tribunal other than the Senate would have to be found; a number of delegates had preferred direct election by the people; and most important of all, it was essential to make the president independent of the legislature.

The first point of the Committee's proposal which was attacked was the Senate's right of choice in the event that no one candidate had an electoral majority. Wilson stated that this would be dangerous because the Senate "will have in fact the appointment of the President, and through his dependence on them, the virtual appointment to offices . . . They are to make treaties . . . and try all impeachments . . . the President will not be the man of the people, as he ought to be, but the Minion of the Senate."

After considerable discussion the proposal was amended so that the House instead of the Senate would cast the decisive vote. Interestingly enough this reflected considerable sentiment in behalf of legislature control, for it was felt that a tie would be the rule rather than the exception and that Congress would in effect exercise the power of executive selection. Hamilton predicted election by the House of Representatives 19 times out of 20; Mason thought it would be 49 times out of 50.

At long last the Committee's report was approved. The decisive factor in influencing the delegates, when many had preferred election by the legislature, was the desire to secure indefinite reeligibility for the president. Under legislative control of the executive, factional contests at election time would have been inevitable. Reeligibility could have been achieved by providing for direct popular vote, but the electoral college plan had the advantage of permitting each state to determine its own suffrage requirements.

The whole question of the method of selecting the executive and of his reeligibility went to the core of the principle of equal and coordinate branches of government. If the system of dual federalism was one unique contribution of the Founding Fathers to the science of political state-craft, the equal and coordinate feature was the other.

On September 8, a "Committee on Stile" was chosen to put the draft document into final shape. In designating the office of the president, the Committee on Detail had previously reported: "the executive power shall be vested in a single person. His style shall be 'the President of the United States' and his title shall be 'His Excellency'." Morris, for the Committee, changed the wording to "the executive power shall be vested in a President of the United States of America. . . ."

The "broad constructionists" among the delegates at the Constitutional Convention and broad constructionists ever since have so interpreted this clause as to make it embody a large grant of discretionary and residual power. They have been supported in their position by the further simple statement in Article II that ". . . he shall take care that the laws be faithfully executed. . . ."

In its final form this is the kind of executive provided for by the Convention of 1787: a president chosen by electors from each state every four years and eligible for re-election; commander-in-chief of the armed forces of the United States; endowed with the power to grant reprieves and pardons for offenses against the nation, to make treaties by and with the consent of the Senate, to appoint ambassadors, judges of the Supreme Court, and so on, with the consent of the Senate, to approve or qualifiedly veto congressional bills. He may require in writing the opinions of heads of executive departments upon the duties relating to their offices; he may call special sessions of congress; he shall receive ambassadors of foreign nations; and "he shall take care that the laws be faithfully executed."

The Wilsonian concept of the presidency had prevailed: government by limited powers and of coordinate departments. The unrestrained legislature and the dependent executive, which existed for a while after the Revolution, had had their day.

In time, the powers conferred upon the president—the message to

congress, the veto, treaty making, and the conduct of foreign policy—
have through constitutional usage, political parties, and forceful leadership transformed the office into what one leading constitutional authority
has termed "the new Presidency." With the years the uniqueness of the
office has been ever more clearly demonstrated. As Harold J. Laski aptly
put it:

> It is not, I think, merely a platitude to say that the essence of the Presi-
> dency is the fact that it is an American institution, that it functions in an
> American environment, that it has been shaped by the forces of American
> history, that it must be judged by American criteria of its response to Ameri-
> can needs.

4

The Transformation of the Constitutional President

EDWARD S. CORWIN

*Occupants of the Presidential office have interpreted its constitutional
foundations in two ways. One interpretation assigns to the executive
branch an autonomous place in the national government; the other assigns it a subordinate status in relation to the legislative branch. Generally speaking, as Corwin suggests, the history of the Presidency has
been marked by aggrandizement. This trend resulted from the strong
leadership exercised by forceful Presidents, such as Washington, Jefferson, Jackson, Lincoln, Wilson and the two Roosevelts. The precedents
they established, the historical shift from a* laissez-faire *government to
one directly involved in promoting economic stability and social justice,
and the emergence of the United States as a world power, have combined
to elevate the Presidency to unprecedented and paramount significance.*

IT IS AN axiom of American history that the Constitution came from the
Framers "a bundle of compromises." Not so generally recognized is the
confirmation lent this observation by those clauses of the Constitution
most nearly affecting the office and powers of the President. The vagueness of the constitutional grants of power to the President has always

Edward S. Corwin, The President: Office and Powers, 1787-1957, *Fourth Revised
Edition (New York: New York University Press, Inc., 1957), pp. 306-313. Reprinted
by permission.*

furnished matter for comment, sometimes favorable, sometimes other-wise, depending on the commentator's bias. "The executive power shall be vested in a President of the United States of America"; "the President shall be Commander-in-Chief of the Army and Navy"; with the advice and consent of the Senate he shall make treaties and appoint to office; he shall have power to "grant pardons for offenses against the United States"; he shall "recommend . . . such measures to Congress as he shall judge necessary and expedient"; and so on and so forth. Yet in order to exercise any of these powers—in order, indeed, to subsist—he must have money, and can get it only when and if Congress appropriates it. Likewise, he is dependent on Congress for the very agencies through which he must ordinarily exercise his powers, and Congress is the judge as to the necessity and propriety of such agencies. Again he is bound to "take care that the laws" that Congress enacts are "faithfully executed"; for this purpose all his powers are in servitude; and Congress has the power to investigate his every official act, and can, by a special procedure, if it finds him guilty of "high crimes and misdemeanors," impeach him and throw him out of office. Moreover, by the standard set by the pre-rogative of the British monarch in 1787, his "executive power" and his power to protect were both seriously curtailed. The power to "declare war" was vested in Congress; the Senate was made a participant in his diplomatic powers; he was given a veto on all legislative acts, but one that the houses can override by a two-thirds vote.

In short, the Constitution reflects the struggle between two con-ceptions of executive power: that it ought always to be subordinate to the supreme legislative power, and that it ought to be, within generous limits, autonomous and self-directing; or, in other terms, the idea that the people are *represented* in the Legislature versus the idea that they are *embodied* in the Executive. Nor has this struggle ever entirely ceased, although on the whole it is the latter theory that has prospered. . . . Taken by and large, the history of the presidency has been a history of aggrandizement.

The office got off to a good start under a very great man. The principle of the Separation of Powers was not yet regarded as forbidding the executive to initate legislation. In the act establishing the State Department Congress itself laid down a "practical construction" of the Constitution that, save for the interregnum of the Reconstruction Period, has left the President absolute master of his official family. A dangerous foreign situation in 1793 brought that family into existence, while it also enabled the President to translate his position as the organ of communication with other governments into a substantive, creative power. Finally, the Whisky Rebellion provided the occasion for the first step in that course of legislation and of presidential action that has long since invested the President, in situations of widespread disorder or threat of it, with powers of dictatorship.

Under Jefferson and the "Virginia School of Presidents" a certain retrogression took place from the notion of presidential autonomy toward that of legislative supremacy. Under Jefferson himself the retreat was theoretical rather than actual. As the founder and leader of the first national party he was able to dominate Congress by personal influence, and it was shown for the first time what accession of strength political skill can bring the presidency. But Jefferson's successors, caught between the upper and nether millstones of their self-abasing conception of the presidency and their lack of personal force, were reduced to official insignificance. The War of 1812 marked the near elimination for the time being of presidential prerogative in the field of foreign relations; the Monroe Doctrine announced to the world at large that opportunities for aggrandizing the presidency from foreign adventuring were to be confined strictly to the Western Hemisphere. Jefferson pronounced the dictum that no President could with safety to our democratic institutions be eligible for a third term, albeit he might nominate his successor; and the successors whom Jefferson himself nominated ratified the ban.

Jackson's presidency was more than a revulsion to earlier ideas: it was a revolution. A new electorate was organized into a new party whose wide ramifications, focusing in the National Convention, rendered its continuance independent of accidents of personality. Guaranteed this powerful and persistent support among the people at large, Jackson extended the doctrine of the President's autonomy to embrace his obligation to the law; constitutional obligation was reduced—or exalted —to the level of moral obligation. At the same time the President's duty to "take care that the laws be faithfully executed" was asserted to comprise the right to read the law for any and every member of the Executive Department; and through a vigorous and expanded use of his veto and removal powers Jackson for the time being made this claim good. Through the latter power, moreover, the Spoils System was for the first time engrafted on the national government, thereby adding one more weapon to the presidential armory.

Except nevertheless for a few unfortunates like John C. Calhoun and Nicholas Biddle, the Jacksonian "dictatorship" was more bark than bite, more proclamation than performance. The Monroe Doctrine, the taboo on a third term, and, what was even more important, the States Rights conception of national legislative power, all set conspicuous landmarks that Jackson himself had not the slightest inclination to disturb. His most outstanding assertions of power, and especially in the field of legislation, were negative and exercised by veto. Moreover, despite the permanency of the party organization reared by his henchmen in every quarter of the Union the prominence of the office during his incumbency was predominantly a reflection of his own energetic personality. When he left office he left behind him a political vacuum that a resuscitated Congress presently filled, and, thanks to the manipulations of the slavery interest, continued to fill—if exception be made of slavery's tool, the sly, pious Polk—till the outbreak of the Civil War.

For all that, the Jacksonian conception of the presidency was not forgotten. Indeed, its champions and its critics contributed about equally to render it more articulate than ever—a fact of the first magnitude when Lincoln became President and found himself confronted with a nation in dissolution. Lincoln's claim to "the war power" was derived from three sources: Jackson's doctrine that *all* the President's powers are autonomous; the Supreme Court's doctrine in *Luther v. Borden* (1849) that insurrection is "war"; and the measures which Pierce and Buchanan had taken in their efforts to put down civil war in Kansas, together with the budget of doctrine which the legal genius of Caleb Cushing had furnished them in justification of their policy.

At first, as we pointed out on an earlier page, Lincoln laid claim only to an *ad interim* war power, one operative only until Congress could ratify and reinforce its measures; but the Supreme Court's sweeping language in the Prize cases (1863) encouraged him to take a more forthright stand, and this, combined with his indisposition to co-operate with Congress, led him to break over constitutional bounds and become a dictator even exceeding the Roman model. Nor was the constitutional corrective applied until after the war was comfortably over, by the Court's decision in *ex parte Milligan* and by Congress's uprising against Johnson. The implication of Lincoln's course that the President has power to meet an emergency without awaiting action by Congress is accordant with the most ancient traditions of Anglo-American law; but when on this implication Lincoln sought to erect a plan of Reconstruction in which the role of the national legislative power was negligible, he brought the presidency in the person of his too zealous apostle Johnson to the verge of disaster. Even so, it fell to Johnson, by escaping impeachment, to demonstrate the impracticability of this medieval method of controlling presidential power. Moreover, it was during his term that the Supreme Court virtually underwrote, in *Mississippi v. Johnson* (1867), Jackson's contention that the President's duty to the Constitution is solely the duty of conscience that his oath imposes.

But again the cyclical character of presidential power demonstrated itself. As from 1809 to 1829, so again from 1865 to 1885 the legislative power became the dominant element of the national government. Indeed, except for the success of Presidents Hayes and Cleveland in using the Army to put down "domestic violence" within the states the period of congressional preponderance reached to the death of McKinley. But meantime Congress by its own headiness had paved the way for the recrudescence of its constitutional rival, by forcing on McKinley the war with Spain. By that act and the consequences that ensued from it the restrictive effect of the Monroe Doctrine on presidential prerogative was seriously undermined. The United States was now a "world power," and presently it found itself involved in a World War.

The great accession to presidential power in recent decades has, however, taken place in the *internal* equally with the *external* field of government, and has been signalized by the breakdown of the two great structural principles of the American Constitutional System, the doctrine of dual federalism and the doctrine of the Separation of Powers; while along with this breakdown has gone an even more fundamental change in popular outlook regarding the purpose and scope of governmental power. I mean, of course, the replacement of the *laissez-faire* theory of government with the idea that government should make itself an *active, reforming* force in the field of economic enterprise, which means necessarily that the *national government* should be active in this way, inasmuch as the field in question has long since come to transcend state lines.

The result for the presidency has been twofold. On the one hand, Presidents have made themselves spokesmen of the altered outlook, have converted their parties to it—a conversion not infrequently accompanied by backsliding—and, with the popular support this obtained, have asserted a powerful legislative initiative. On the other hand, Congress, in responding to the President's leadership in its own peculiar field, has found it convenient to aggrandize his executive role enormously, by delegating to him the power to supplement its measures by a type of sub-legislation called "administrative regulations." Not all this delegated power, it is true, has gone to the President, but a vast proportion of it has; and it constitutes a realm of presidential power of which the

Framers had little prevision, although it began to appear in the field of foreign relations even as early as Washington's second administration.

The first exponent of the new presidency was Theodore Roosevelt, but his achievement was to some extent negated by faults of method. Woodrow Wilson was enabled by the advantage of having critically observed his predecessor, by his knowledge of political methods abroad, by a taste for institution-building, which was later to divert him into an abortive effort at world organization, and finally by the opportunity afforded by our entrance into the First World War, to illustrate on an unprecedented scale both the new roles of the President—that of legislative leader and that of recipient of delegated legislative power. The First World War was prosecuted for the most part under laws drafted under the appraising eye of the President and conferring on him far greater powers than those Lincoln had exercised as Commander-in-Chief.

But it is the second Roosevelt who beyond all twentieth-century Presidents put the stamp both of *personality* and *crisis* on the presidency. In the solution of the problems of an economic crisis—"a crisis greater than war"—he claimed for the national government in general and for the President in particular powers hitherto exercised only on the justification of war. Then when the greatest crisis in the history of our international relations arose he imparted to the President's diplomatic powers new extension, now without consulting Congress, now with Congress's approval; and when at last we entered the Second World War he endowed the precedents of both the Civil War and the First World War with unprecedented scope.

The presidency of this present year of grace, so far as it is explicable in terms of American constitutional law and theory, is the product of the following factors: (1) social acceptance of the idea that government should be active and reformist, rather than simply protective of the established order of things; (2) the breakdown of the principle of dual federalism in the field of Congress's legislative powers; (3) the breakdown of the principle of the Separation of Powers as defining the relation of President and Congress in lawmaking; (4) the breakdown of the corollary principle that the legislature may not delegate its powers; and (5) the impact of the President's power as Commander-in-Chief and the organ of foreign relationship of two world wars and the vastly enlarged role of the United States in the international field.

Does the presidency, then, in the light of these facts, constitute a standing menace to popular government and to those conceptions of personal liberty to which popular government is, in part, traceable? So far as concerns popular government in the sense of majority rule, the exact contrary is the case: all the developments named are the direct consequence of democracy's emergence from the constitutional chrysalis. That, on the other hand, these developments leave private and personal rights in the same strong position as they once enjoyed would be quite impossible to maintain. Nor is it feasible in this connection to distinguish too acutely between the property and other rights. Not only in the past, but today as well, the property right is the right best capable of holding its own against political power. This is the principal lesson to be drawn from the history of Liberalism.

As matters have stood till the other day, presidential power has been at times dangerously *personalized,* and this in two senses: first, that the leadership that it affords was dependent altogether on the accident of personality, against which our haphazard method of selecting Presidents offers no guarantee; and, secondly, that there is no governmental body that could be relied on to give the President independent advice and that he was nevertheless bound to consult. As a remedy calculated to meet both phases of the problem I have suggested a new type of Cabinet. At least, if a solution is to be sought in *institutional* terms, it must consist in *stabilizing* in some way or other the relationship between President and Congress.

Recent developments, however, may have relegated my proposal, even if it ever had any real prospect of acceptance, to the limbo of happy untried ideas—happy, perhaps, because untried. In the "Institutionalized Presidency" the President becomes merged with—albeit not submerged in—a cluster of institutions designed to base government in the national area on conference and consensus. The "Institutionalized Presidency" is the contribution of Congress and of recent Presidents, but particularly of President Eisenhower, whose temperament, training, and needs it obviously meets. But is it a permanent structure? In our "world in transition" no confident prediction can be safely vouchsafed. The incalculables are too many and too formidable.

▓▓▓▓▓▓▓▓▓▓▓▓▓▓▓▓▓▓

PRESIDENTS VIEW THEIR OFFICE

Through most of the nation's history, Presidents have subscribed to one of two theories on the limits of power in the executive branch of the government. The enlarged, expansive view is that the powers of the office are not restricted to those specifically enumerated in the Constitution, but that there is an "undefined residuum" of power which may be tapped in the national interest. Conversely, the restricted or legalistic conception is that the President is bound by the specifically enumerated constitutional limitations and must scrupulously observe the jurisdictional lines between the various branches of government. In short, one theory envisages the President as an activist occupying the center of power, while the other sees him in a passive role, carefully adhering to constitutional niceties.

A President's conception of his office has naturally influenced the manner in which he exercised power. Adherence to the broad interpretation is conducive to a vigorous exercise of leadership, while a narrow, "strictly constitutional" view inhibits him, since such a value is congenial to the diminution of power. In contemporary America, however, the passive approach has become as anachronistic as the horse and buggy. The tremendous proliferation of governmental responsibilities, both in domestic and in foreign affairs, demands that the modern President be an activist. Any Chief Executive, whether Democrat or Republican, must regard his office in a "large" manner. The question is not whether the President will be involved in the concerns of the times, but rather how capable will he be in responding effectively to their complex demands.

I

The Stewardship Doctrine

In a succinct statement of the enlarged and expansive concept of the Presidency, Theodore Roosevelt argued that in order to promote the national welfare the President may exercise any power which is not expressly forbidden by the Constitution. Such a President does not usurp power, he maintained, but acts in the best interests of the people.

. . . THE MOST IMPORTANT factor in getting the right spirit in my Administration, next to the insistence upon courage, honesty, and a genuine democracy of desire to serve the plain people, was my insistence upon the theory that the executive power was limited only by specific restrictions and prohibitions appearing in the Constitution or imposed by the Congress under its Constitutional powers. My view was that every executive officer, and above all every executive officer in high position, was a steward of the people bound actively and affirmatively to do all he could for the people, and not to content himself with the negative merit of keeping his talents undamaged in a napkin. I declined to adopt the view that what was imperatively necessary for the Nation could not be done by the President unless he could find some specific authorization to do it. My belief was that it was not only his right but his duty to do anything that the needs of the Nation demanded unless such action was forbidden by the Constitution or by the laws. Under this interpretation of executive power I did and caused to be done many things not previously done by the President and the heads of the departments. I did not usurp power, but I did greatly broaden the use of executive power. In other words, I acted for the public welfare, I acted for the common well-being of all our people, whenever and in whatever manner was necessary, unless prevented by direct constitutional or legislative prohibition. I did not care a rap for the mere form and show of power; I cared immensely for the use that could be made of the substance. . . .

Theodore Roosevelt, An Autobiography *(N.Y.: Charles Scribner's Sons, 1924), p. 357. Copyright 1913 by Charles Scribner's Sons. Reprinted by permission.*

2

A Restricted View of the Office

WILLIAM HOWARD TAFT

*William Howard Taft's approach to the Presidency, based on a narrow,
legalistic, and strictly constitutional view, was in direct contrast to that
of his predecessor. There is, he said, "no undefined residuum of power"
which the President can draw upon, and the Roosevelt doctrine, he contended, was fallacious and dangerous.*

WHILE IT IS important to mark out the exclusive field of jurisdiction of
each branch of the government, Legislative, Executive and Judicial, it
should be said that in the proper working of the government there must
be cooperation of all branches, and without a willingness of each branch
to perform its function, there will follow a hopeless obstruction to the
progress of the whole government. Neither branch can compel the other
to affirmative action, and each branch can greatly hinder the other in the
attainment of the object of its activities and the exercise of its discretion.
. . . The true view of the Executive function is, as I conceive it,
that the President can exercise no power which cannot be fairly and
reasonably traced to some specific grant of power or justly implied and
included within such express grant as proper and necessary to its exercise. Such specific grant must be either in the Federal Constitution or
in an act of Congress passed in pursuance thereof. There is no undefined
residuum of power which he can exercise because it seems to him to be
in the public interest, and there is nothing in the Neagle case and its
definition of a law of the United States, or in other precedents, warrant-
ing such an inference. The grants of Executive power are necessarily in
general terms in order not to embarrass the Executive within the field of
action plainly marked for him, but his jurisdiction must be justified and
vindicated by affirmative constitutional or statutory provision, or it does
not exist. There have not been wanting, however, eminent men in high
public office holding a different view and who have insisted upon the

*William Howard Taft, Our Chief Magistrate and His Powers (New York: Columbia
University Press, 1925), pp. 138-140. Copyright 1916 by Columbia University Press.
Reprinted by permission.*

necessity for an undefined residuum of Executive power in the public interest. They have not been confined to the present generation.

. . . I may add that Mr. Roosevelt, by way of illustrating his meaning as to the differing usefulness of Presidents, divides the Presidents into two classes, and designates them as "Lincoln Presidents" and "Buchanan Presidents." In order more fully to illustrate his division of Presidents on their merits, he places himself in the Lincoln class of Presidents, and me in the Buchanan class. The identification of Mr. Roosevelt with Mr. Lincoln might otherwise have escaped notice, because there are many differences between the two, presumably superficial, which would give the impartial student of history a different impression. It suggests a story which a friend of mine told of his little daughter Mary. As he came walking home after a business day, she ran out from the house to greet him, all aglow with the importance of what she wished to tell him. She said, "Papa, I am the best scholar in the class." The father's heart throbbed with pleasure as he inquired, "Why, Mary, you surprise me. When did the teacher tell you? This afternoon?" "Oh, no," Mary's reply was, "the teacher didn't tell me—I just noticed it myself."

My judgment is that the view of Mr. Garfield and Mr. Roosevelt, ascribing an undefined residuum of power to the President is an unsafe doctrine and that it might lead under emergencies to results of an arbitrary character, doing irremediable injustice to private right. The mainspring of such a view is that the Executive is charged with responsibility for the welfare of all the people in a general way, that he is to play the part of a Universal Providence and set all things right, and that anything that in his judgment will help the people he ought to do, unless he is expressly forbidden not to do it. The wide field of action that this would give to the Executive one can hardly limit.

3

A Model for Assertive Leadership

WOODROW WILSON

In his book, Congressional Government, *published in 1885, Woodrow Wilson deplored the primacy of Congress, and regretted that the American system of government did not afford the President the opportunities for leadership available to the British Prime Minister. By 1907, however, doubtless influenced by the example of President Roosevelt, he came to believe that dynamic and vigorous White House leadership was possible within the existing framework of the American governmental system. Wilson now maintained, in his* Constitutional Government in the United States, *that the President was the leader of his party as well as of the nation, and that his paramount role in foreign relations elevated him to a position of unique importance.*

. . . HE [THE PRESIDENT] cannot escape being the leader of his party except by incapacity and lack of personal force, because he is at once the choice of the party and of the nation. He is the party nominee, and the only party nominee for whom the whole nation votes. Members of the House and Senate are representatives of localities, are voted for only by sections of voters, or by local bodies of electors like the members of the state legislatures. There is no national party choice except that of President. No one else represents the people as a whole, exercising a national choice; and inasmuch as his strictly executive duties are in fact subordinated, so far at any rate as all detail is concerned, the President represents not so much the party's governing efficiency as its controlling ideals and principles. He is not so much part of its organization as its vital link of connection with the thinking nation. He can dominate his party by being spokesman for the real sentiment and purpose of the country, by giving direction to opinion, by giving the country at once the information and the statements of policy which will enable it to form its judgments alike of parties and of men.

For he is also the political leader of the nation, or has it in his choice to be. The nation as a whole has chosen him, and is conscious that it has no other political spokesman. His is the only national voice in affairs. Let him once win the admiration and confidence of the country, and no other single force can withstand him, no combination of forces will easily overpower him. His position takes the imagination of the country. He is the representative of no constituency, but of the whole people. When he speaks in his true character, he speaks for no special interest. If he rightly interpret the national thought and boldly insist upon it, he is irresistible; and the country never feels the zest of action so much as when its President is of such insight and calibre. Its instinct is for unified action, and it craves a single leader. It is for this reason that it will often prefer to choose a man rather than a party. A President whom it trusts can not only lead it, but form it to his own views.

It is the extraordinary isolation imposed upon the President by our system that makes the character and opportunity of his office so extraordinary. In him are centered both opinion and party. He may stand, if he will, a little outside party and insist as if it were upon the general opinion. It is with the instinctive feeling that it is upon occasion such a man that the country wants that nominating conventions will often nominate men who are not their acknowledged leaders, but only such men as the country would like to see lead both its parties. The President may also, if he will, stand within the party counsels and use the advantage of his power and personal force to control its actual programs. He may be both the leader of his party and the leader of the nation, or he may be one or the other. If he lead the nation, his party can hardly resist him. His office is anything he has the sagacity and force to make it.

That is the reason why it has been one thing at one time, another at another. The Presidents who have not made themselves leaders have lived no more truly on that account in the spirit of the Constitution than those whose force has told in the determination of law and policy. No doubt Andrew Jackson overstepped the bounds meant to be set to the authority of his office. It was certainly in direct contravention of the spirit of the Constitution that he should have refused to respect and execute decisions of the Supreme Court of the United States, and no serious student of our history can righteously condone what he did in such matters on the ground that his intentions were upright and his principles pure. But the Constitution of the United States is not a mere lawyers' document: it is a vehicle of life, and its spirit it always the spirit of the age. Its prescriptions are clear and we know what they are; a written document makes lawyers of us all, and our duty as citizens should make us conscientious lawyers, reading the text of the Constitution without subtlety or sophistication; but life is always your last and most authoritative critic.

Some of our Presidents have deliberately held themselves off from using the full power they might legitimately have used, because of conscientious scruples, because they were more theorists than statesmen. They have held the strict literary theory of the Constitution, the Whig theory, the Newtonian theory, and have acted as if they thought that Pennsylvania Avenue should have been even longer than it is; that there should be no intimate communication of any kind between the Capitol and the White House; that the President as a man was no more at liberty to lead the houses of Congress by persuasion than he was at liberty as President to dominate them by authority,—supposing that he had, what he has not, authority enough to dominate them. But the makers of the Constitution were not enacting Whig theory, they were not making laws with the expectation that, not the laws themselves, but their opinions, known by future historians to lie back of them, should govern the constitutional action of the country. They were statesmen, not pedants, and their laws are sufficient to keep us to the paths they set us upon. The President is at liberty, both in law and conscience, to be as big a man as he can. His capacity will set the limit; and if Congress be overborne by him, it will be no fault of the makers of the Constitution,—it will be from no lack of constitutional powers on its part, but only because the President has the nation behind him, and Congress has not. He has no means of compelling Congress except through public opinion. . . .

One of the greatest of the President's powers I have not yet spoken of at all: his control, which is very absolute, of the foreign relations of the nation. The initiative in foreign affairs, which the President possesses without any restriction whatever, is virtually the power to control them absolutely. The President cannot conclude a treaty with a foreign power without the consent of the Senate, but he may guide every step of diplomacy, and to guide diplomacy is to determine what treaties must be made, if the faith and prestige of the government are to be maintained. He need disclose no step of negotiation until it is complete, and when in any critical matter it is completed the government is virtually committed. Whatever its disinclination, the Senate may feel itself committed also.

I have not dwelt upon this power of the President, because it has been decisively influential in determining the character and influence of the office at only two periods in our history; at the very first, when the government was young and had so to use its incipient force as to win the respect of the nations into whose family it had thrust itself, and in our own day when the results of the Spanish War, the ownership of distant possessions, and many sharp struggles for foreign trade make it necessary that we should turn our best talents to the task of dealing firmly, wisely, and justly with political and commercial rivals. The President can never again be the mere domestic figure he has been throughout so large a part of our history. The nation has risen to the first rank in power and resources. The other nations of the world look askance upon her, half in envy, half in fear, and wonder with a deep anxiety what she will do with her vast strength. They receive the frank professions of men like Mr. John Hay, whom we wholly trusted, with a grain of salt, and doubt what we were sure of, their truthfulness and sincerity, suspecting a hidden design under every utterance he makes. Our President must always, henceforth, be one of the great powers of the world, whether he act greatly and wisely or not, and the best statesmen we can produce will be needed to fill the office of Secretary of State. We have but begun to see the presidential office in this light; but it is the light which will more and more beat upon it, and more and more determine its character and its effect upon the politics of the nation. We can never hide our President again as a mere domestic officer. We can never again see him the mere executive he was in the thirties and forties. He must stand always at the front of our affairs, and the office will be as big and as influential as the man who occupies it.

How is it possible to sum up the duties and influence of such an office in such a system in comprehensive terms which will cover all its changeful aspects? In the view of the makers of the Constitution the President was to be legal executive; perhaps the leader of the nation; certainly not the leader of the party, at any rate while in office. But by the operation of forces inherent in the very nature of government he has become all three, and by inevitable consequence the most heavily burdened officer in the world. No other man's day is so full as his, so full of the responsibilities which tax mind and conscience alike and demand an inexhaustible vitality. The mere task of making appointments to office, which the Constitution imposes upon the President, has come near to breaking some of our Presidents down, because it is a never-ending task in a civil service not yet put upon a professional footing, confused with short terms of office, always forming and dissolving. And in proportion as the President ventures to use his opportunity to lead opinion and act as spokesman of the people in affairs the people stand ready to overwhelm him by running to him with every question, great and small. They are as eager to have him settle a literary question as a political; hear him as acquiescently with regard to matters of special expert knowledge as with regard to public affairs, and call upon him to quiet all troubles by his personal intervention. Men of ordinary physique and discretion cannot be Presidents and live, if the strain be not somehow relieved. We shall be obliged always to be picking our chief magistrates from among wise and prudent athletes—a small class. . . .

4

". . . It Is Preeminently a Place of Moral Leadership . . ."

FRANKLIN D. ROOSEVELT

During the twelve years between the Wilson administration and the second Roosevelt, the Presidency was occupied by men with a restricted view of their office. In 1933, with Franklin D. Roosevelt in the White House, the activist theory again came to the fore. Shortly before his election, he expressed his views on presidential leadership, and during his tenure, he translated them into action.

. . . THE PRESIDENCY IS not merely an administrative office. That's the least of it. It is more than an engineering job, efficient or inefficient. It is preeminently a place of moral leadership. All our great Presidents were leaders of thought at times when certain historic ideas in the life of the nation had to be clarified. Washington personified the idea of federal union. Jefferson practically originated the party system as we know it by opposing the democratic theory to the republicanism of Hamilton. This theory was reaffirmed by Jackson. Two great principles of our government were forever put beyond question by Lincoln. Cleveland, coming into office following an era of great political corruption, typified rugged honesty. T.R. and Wilson were both moral leaders, each in his

Anne O'Hare McCormick, *"Roosevelt's View of the Big Job,"* New York Times Magazine *(September 11, 1932), p. 2.* © *1932 by The New York Times Company. Reprinted by permission.*

own way and for his own time, who used the Presidency as a pulpit.

Isn't that what the office is—a superb opportunity for reapplying, applying in new conditions, the simple rules of human conduct we always go back to? I stress the modern application, because we are always moving on; the technical and economic environment changes, and never so quickly as now. Without leadership alert and sensitive to change, we are bogged up or lose our way, as we have lost it in the past decade. . . .

5

Lobbyist for All the People

HARRY S TRUMAN

At a dinner commemorating his birthday in 1954, Harry S Truman articulated his presidential credo as he had done on many other occasions. The Chief Executive he declared, must exercise broad leadership, for he is the only lobbyist in Washington for all the people. He must resist legislative encroachments on his power because the nation would suffer if that power were enfeebled. Conflict between the executive and legislative branches is inherent in our constitutional system, he argued, and no President should shrink from asserting his prerogatives.

. . . [THE PRESIDENCY] IS the greatest office in the history of the world. . . .

When the founding fathers outlined the Presidency in Article II of the Constitution, they left a great many details out and vague. I think they relied on the experience of the nation to fill in the outlines. The office of chief executive has grown with the progress of this great republic. It has responded to the many demands that our complex society has made upon the Government. It has given our nation a means of meeting our greatest emergencies. Today, it is one of the most important factors in our leadership of the free world.

Many diverse elements entered into the creation of the office, springing, as it did, from the parent idea of the separation of powers.

There was the firm conviction of such powerful and shrewd minds as that of John Adams that the greatest protection against unlimited power lay in an executive secured against the encroachment of the national assembly. Then there were the fears of those who suspected a plot to establish a monarchy on these shores. Others believed that the experience under the Confederation showed above all the need of stability through a strong central administration. Finally, there was the need for compromise among these and many other views.

The result was a compromise—a compromise which that shrewd observer, Alexis de Tocqueville, over 120 years ago, believed would not work. He thought that the Presidential office was too weak. The President, he thought, was at the mercy of Congress. The President could recommend, to be sure, he thought, but the President had no power and the Congress had the power. The Congress could disregard his recommendations, overrule his vetoes, reject his nominations. De Tocqueville thought that no man of parts, worthy of leadership, would accept so feeble a role.

This was not a foolish view and there was much in our early history which tended to bear it out. But there is a power in the course of events which plays its own part. In this case again, Justice Holmes' epigram proved true. He said a page of history is worth a volume of logic. And as the pages of history were written they unfolded powers in the Presidency not explicitly found in Article II of the Constitution.

In the first place, the President became the leader of a political party. The party under his leadership had to be dominant enough to put him in office. This political party leadership was the last thing the Constitution contemplated. The President's election was not intended to be mixed up in the hurly-burly of partisan politics. . . . The people were to choose wise and respected men who would meet in calm seclusion and choose a President and the runner-up would be Vice President.

All of this went by the board—though most of the original language remains in the Constitution. Out of the struggle and tumult of the political arena a new and different President emerged—the man who led a political party to victory and retained in his hands the power of party leadership. That is, he retained it like the sword Excalibur, if he could wrest it from the scabbard and wield it.

Another development was connected with the first. As the President came to be elected by the whole people, he became responsible to the whole people. I used to say the only lobbyist the whole people had in Washington was the President of the United States. Our whole people looked to him for leadership, and not confined within the limits of a written document. Every hope and every fear of his fellow citizens, almost every aspect of their welfare and activity, falls within the scope of his concern—indeed, it falls within the scope of his duty. Only one who has held that office can really appreciate that. It is the President's responsibility to look at all questions from the point of view of the whole people. His written and spoken word commands national and often international attention.

These powers which are not explicitly written into the Constitution are powers which no President can pass on to his successor. They go only to him who can take and use them. However, it is these powers, quite as much as those enumerated in Article II of the Constitution which make the Presidential system unique. . . .

For it is through the use of these great powers that leadership arises, events are molded and administrations take on their character. Their use can make a Jefferson or a Lincoln Administration; their non-use can make a Buchanan or a Grant Administration.

Moreover, a study of these aspects of our governmental and political history will save us from self-righteousness—from taking a holier than thou attitude toward other nations. For brilliant and enduring as were the minds of the architects of our Constitution, they did not devise a foolproof system to protect us against the disaster of a weak government—that is, government unable to face and resolve—one way or another—pressing national problems. Indeed, in some respects, the separation of powers requires stronger executive leadership than does the parliamentary and cabinet system.

As Justice Brandeis used to say, the separation of powers was not devised to promote efficiency in government. In fact, it was devised to prevent one form of deficiency—absolutism or dictatorship. By making the Congress separate and independent in the exercise of its powers, and the executive separate and independent in the exercise of its powers, a certain amount of political conflict was built into the Constitution. For the price of independence is eternal vigilance and a good deal of struggle. And this is not a bad thing—on the contrary, it is a good thing for the preservation of the liberty of the people—if it does not become conflict just for its own sake.

I've always said that the President who didn't have a fight with the Congress wasn't any good anyhow. And that is no reflection on the Congress. They are always looking after their rights. You needn't doubt that.

Having been in these two branches of government, legislative and executive, I think I am expressing a considered and impartial opinion in saying that the powers of the President are much more difficult to exercise and to preserve from encroachment than those of the Congress. In part, this comes from the difficulty of the problems of our time, and from the fact that upon the President falls the responsibility of obtaining action, timely and adequate to meet the nation's needs. Whatever the Constitution says, he is held responsible for any disaster which may come.

And so a successful administration is one of strong Presidential leadership. Weak leadership—or no leadership—produces failure and often disaster.

This does not come from the inherent incapacity of the people of the nation. It is inherent in legislative government where there is no executive strong and stable enough to rally the people to a sustained effort of will and prepared to use its power of party control to the fullest extent.

Today, also, one of the great responsibilities and opportunities of the President is to lead and inspire public opinion. The words of a President carry great weight. His acts carry even more weight.

All of us remember the words of Franklin D. Roosevelt in his first inaugural address which did so much to rally the spirit of a nation struggling through the depths of a depression. He said "the only thing we have to fear is fear itself." These words, however, would have had little effect if President Roosevelt had not backed them up by action. Following that speech, President Roosevelt plunged into a vigorous course, striking at the depression on all fronts. He backed his words by his action, and words and action restored the faith of the nation in its government and in its form of government, too.

Today, there is the same need for a similar combination of words and action concerning the hysteria about communism. Our country has acted firmly and resolutely to hold Communist imperialism in check. Nevertheless, that concern has created fear and fear has been played upon by persons who see in it an easy way to influence votes. There is no dispute any more that this unreasonable fear exists. The leaders of both political parties have acknowledged it. I do not wish to go into this subject at length tonight. I have talked a good deal about it of late, and most recently at Westminster College in Missouri where Winston Churchill made his famous Iron Curtain speech. We all know the corrosive effect of this hysteria and the dangers it holds.

But, as I have said, the office of the Presidency is the one office of our Government to which all the people turn when they are beset by fears like these. It is to the President that they look to say a firm "No" to those who wish to destroy others through fear and innuendo. It is his duty to defend the unjustly accused and demonstrate in the executive branch of the Government that the ancient principles of fair play and decency prevail all the time. By such deeds and acts the Presidency can reassure the nation and stem the growth of hysteria.

Again, we see today history repeating itself as the legislative branch of the Government, under the overshadowing fear of communism, expands its functions and activities into the very center of the power of the executive branch.

The President is responsible for the administration of his office. And that means for the administration of the entire executive branch. It is not the business of Congress to run the agencies of government for the President.

Unless this principle is observed, it is impossible to have orderly government. The legislative power will ooze into the executive offices. It will influence and corrupt the decisions of the executive branch. It will affect promotions and transfers. It will warp and twist policies.

Not only does the President cease to be master in his own house, but the whole house of government becomes one which has no master. The power of decision then rests only in the legislative branch, and the legislative branch by its very nature is not equipped to perform these executive functions.

To this kind of encroachment it is the duty of the President to say firmly and flatly "No, you can't do it." The investigative power of Congress is not limitless. It extends only so far as to permit the Congress to acquire the information that it honestly needs to exercise its legislative functions. Exercised beyond those limits, it becomes a manifestation of unconstitutional power. It raises the threat of legislative dictatorship and that's the worst dictatorship in the world.

Our nation was once almost torn apart by such an expansion of Congressional power. That was in the age of President Johnson, when the Radical Republicans of that time tried to take over the functions of the President. But we cannot afford such an attack on the Presidency by today's version of the Radical Republicans.

Today the perils and problems which threaten us and our allies make all the difficulties of the Reconstruction period—that tragic era— seem rather pale. Today the tasks of leadership falling upon the President spring not only from our national problems but from those of the whole world. Today that leadership will determine whether our Government will function effectively, and upon its functioning depends the survival of each of us and also on that depends the survival of the free world, if I may be so bold as to say that.

And today our Government cannot function properly unless it follows the provisions of the Constitution. Our Government cannot function properly unless the President is master in his own house and unless the executive departments and agencies of the Government, including the armed forces, are responsible to the President. . . .

6

"Today a Restricted Concept of the Presidency Is Not Enough"

JOHN F. KENNEDY

During his election campaign, John F. Kennedy cogently expressed his views on the requirements for presidential leadership. Not since Wilson had a candidate spoken so meaningfully on the subject. The President, he declared, should immerse himself completely in both the political process and the affairs of state, and should use all the powers constitutionally available to him as well as those legitimate powers available apart from the Constitution. He must exercise political and party leadership as the instruments of effective national authority, and address himself with conviction and compassion to the major problems challenging the nation at home and abroad.

THE MODERN PRESIDENTIAL campaign covers every issue in and out of the platform from cranberries to creation. But the public is rarely alerted to a candidate's views about the central issue on which all the rest turn. That central issue—and the point of my comments this noon—is not the farm problem or defense or India. It is the presidency itself.

Of course a candidate's views on specific policies are important, but Theodore Roosevelt and William Howard Taft shared policy views with entirely different results in the White House. Of course it is important to elect a good man with good intentions, but Woodrow Wilson and Warren G. Harding were both good men of good intentions; so were

Congressional Record, 86th Congress, 2nd Session (January 18, 1960), A353-354.

Lincoln and Buchanan; but there is a Lincoln Room in the White House and no Buchanan Room.

The history of this Nation—its brightest and its bleakest pages— has been written largely in terms of the different views our Presidents have had of the Presidency itself. This history ought to tell us that the American people in 1960 have an imperative right to know what any man bidding for the Presidency thinks about the place he is bidding for, whether he is aware of and willing to use the powerful resources of that office; whether his model will be Taft or Roosevelt, Wilson or Harding.

Not since the days of Woodrow Wilson has any candidate spoken on the Presidency itself before the votes have been irrevocably cast. Let us hope that the 1960 campaign, in addition to discussing the familiar issues where our positions too often blur, will also talk about the Presidency itself, as an instrument for dealing with those issues, as an office with varying roles, powers, and limitations.

During the past 8 years, we have seen one concept of the Presidency at work. Our needs and hopes have been eloquently stated—but the initiative and follow-through have too often been left to others. And too often his own objectives have been lost by the President's failure to over- ride objections from within his own party, in the Congress or even in his Cabinet.

The American people in 1952 and 1956 may have preferred this detached, limited concept of the Presidency after 20 years of fast-moving, creative Presidential rule. Perhaps historians will regard this as neces- sarily one of those frequent periods of consolidation, a time to draw breath, to recoup our national energy. To quote the state of the Union message: "No Congress . . . on surveying the state of the Nation, has met with a more pleasing prospect than that which appears at the present time."

Unfortunately this is not Mr. Eisenhower's last message to the Con- gress, but Calvin Coolidge's. He followed to the White House Mr. Hard- ing, whose sponsor declared very frankly that the times did not demand a first-rate President. If true, the times and the man met.

But the question is what do the times—and the people—demand for the next 4 years in the White House?

They demand a vigorous proponent of the national interest—not a passive broker for conflicting private interests. They demand a man capable of acting as the commander in chief of the Grand Alliance, not merely a bookkeeper who feels that his work is done when the numbers on the balance sheet come out even. They demand that he be the head of a responsible party, not rise so far above politics as to be invisible—a man who will formulate and fight for legislative policies, not be a casual bystander to the legislative process.

Today a restricted concept of the Presidency is not enough. For beneath today's surface gloss of peace and prosperity are increasingly dangerous, unsolved, long-postponed problems—problems that will inevitably explode to the surface during the next 4 years of the next administration—the growing missile gap, the rise of Communist China, the despair of the underdeveloped nations, the explosive situations in Berlin and in the Formosa Straits, the deterioration of NATO, the lack of an arms control agreement, and all the domestic problems of our farms, cities, and schools.

This administration has not faced up to these and other problems. Much has been said—but I am reminded of the old Chinese proverb: "There is a great deal of noise on the stairs but nobody comes into the room."

The President's state of the Union message reminded me of the exhortation from "King Lear" that goes: "I will do such things—what they are I know not . . . but they shall be the wonders of the earth."

In the decade that lies ahead—in the challenging revolutionary sixties—the American Presidency will demand more than ringing manifestoes issued from the rear of the battle. It will demand that the President place himself in the very thick of the fight, that he care passionately about the fate of the people he leads, that he be willing to serve them at the risk of incurring their momentary displeasure.

Whatever the political affiliation of our next President, whatever his views may be on all the issues and problems that rush in upon us, he must above all be the Chief Executive in every sense of the word. He must be prepared to exercise the fullest powers of his office—all that are specified and some that are not. He must master complex problems as well as receive one-page memorandums. He must originate action as well as study groups. He must reopen the channels of communication between the world of thought and the seat of power.

Ulysses Grant considered the President "a purely administrative officer." If he administered the Government departments efficiently, delegated his functions smoothly, and performed his ceremonies of state with decorum and grace, no more was to be expected of him. But that is not the place the Presidency was meant to have in American life. The President is alone, at the top—the loneliest job there is, as Harry Truman has said.

If there is destructive dissension among the services, he alone can step in and straighten it out—instead of waiting for unanimity. If administrative agencies are not carrying out their mandate—if a brushfire threatens some part of the globe—he alone can act, without waiting for the Congress. If his farm program fails, he alone deserves the blame, not his Secretary of Agriculture.

"The President is at liberty, both in law and conscience, to be as big a man as he can." So wrote Prof. Woodrow Wilson. But President Woodrow Wilson discovered that to be a big man in the White House inevitably brings cries of dictatorship.

So did Lincoln and Jackson and the two Roosevelts. And so may the next occupant of that office, if he is the man the times demand. But how much better it would be, in the turbulent sixties, to have a Roosevelt or a Wilson than to have another James Buchanan, cringing in the White House, afraid to move.

Nor can we afford a Chief Executive who is praised primarily for what he did not do, the disasters he prevented, the bills he vetoed—a President wishing his subordinates would produce more missiles or build more schools. We will need instead what the Constitution envisioned: a Chief Executive who is the vital center of action in our whole scheme of Government.

This includes the legislative process as well. The President cannot afford—for the sake of the office as well as the Nation—to be another Warren G. Harding, described by one backer as a man who "would, when elected, sign whatever bill the Senate sent him—and not send bills for the Senate to pass." Rather he must know when to lead the Congress, when to consult it and when he should act alone.

Having served 14 years in the legislative branch, I would not look with favor upon its domination by the Executive. Under our government of "power as the rival of power," to use Hamilton's phrase, Congress must not surrender its responsibilities. But neither should it dominate. However large its share in the formulation of domestic programs, it is the President alone who must make the major decisions of our foreign policy.

That is what the Constitution wisely commands. And, even domestically, the President must initiate policies and devise laws to meet the needs of the Nation. And he must be prepared to use all the resources of his office to insure the enactment of that legislation—even when conflict is the result.

By the end of his term Theodore Roosevelt was not popular in the

Congress—particularly when he criticized an amendment to the Treasury appropriation which forbade the use of Secret Service men to investigate Congressmen.

And the feeling was mutual, Roosevelt saying: "I do not much admire the Senate, because it is such a helpless body when efficient work is to be done."

And Woodrow Wilson was even more bitter after his frustrating quarrels. Asked if he might run for the Senate in 1920, he replied: "Outside of the United States, the Senate does not amount to a damn. And inside the United States the Senate is mostly despised. They haven't had a thought down there in 50 years."

But, however bitter their farewells, the facts of the matter are that Roosevelt and Wilson did get things done—not only through their Executive powers but through the Congress as well. Calvin Coolidge, on the other hand, departed from Washington with cheers of Congress still ringing in his ears. But when his World Court bill was under fire on Capitol Hill he sent no messages, gave no encouragement to the bill's leaders, and paid little or no attention to the whole proceeding—and the cause of world justice was set back.

To be sure, Coolidge had held the usual White House breakfasts with congressional leaders—but they were aimed, as he himself said, at "good fellowship," not a discussion of "public business." And at his press conferences, according to press historians, where he preferred to talk about the local flower show and its exhibits, reporters who finally extracted from him a single sentence—"I'm against that bill"—would rush to file tongue-in-cheek dispatches, proclaiming that: "President Coolidge, in a fighting mood, today served notice on Congress that he intended to combat, with all the resources at his command, the pending bill. . . ."

But in the coming years we will need a real fighting mood in the White House—a man who will not retreat in the face of pressure from his congressional leaders—who will not let down those supporting his views on the floor. Divided Government over the past 6 years has only been further confused by this lack of legislative leadership. To restore it next year will help restore purpose to both the Presidency and the Congress.

The facts of the matter are that legislative leadership is not possible without party leadership, in the most political sense—and Mr. Eisenhower prefers to stay above politics (although a weekly news magazine last fall reported the startling news, and I quote, that "President Eisenhower is emerging as a major political figure"). When asked, early in his first term, how he liked the "game of politics," he replied with a frown that his questioner was using a derogatory phrase. "Being President," he said, "is a very great experience . . . but the word 'politics' . . . I have no great liking for that."

But no President, it seems to me, can escape politics. He has not only been chosen by the Nation—he has been chosen by his party. And if he insists that he is "President of all the people" and should, therefore, offend none of them—if he blurs the issues and differences between the parties—if he neglects the party machinery and avoids his party's leadership—then he has not only weakened the political party as an instrument of the democratic process—he has dealt a blow to the democratic process itself.

I prefer the example of Abe Lincoln, who loved politics with the passion of a born practitioner. For example, he waited up all night in 1863 to get the crucial returns on the Ohio governorship. When the Unionist candidate was elected, Lincoln wired: "Glory God in the highest. Ohio has saved the Nation."

But the White House is not only the center of political leadership. It must be the center of moral leadership—a "bully pulpit," as Theodore Roosevelt described it. For only the President represents the national interest. And upon him alone converge all the needs and aspirations of all parts of the country, all departments of the Government, all nations of the world.

It is not enough merely to represent prevailing sentiment—to follow McKinley's practice, as described by Joe Cannon, of "keeping his ear so close to the ground he got it full of grasshoppers." We will need in the sixties a President who is willing and able to summon his national constituency to its finest hour—to alert the people to our dangers and our opportunities—to demand of them the sacrifices that will be necessary. Despite the increasing evidence of a lost national purpose and a soft national will, F.D.R.'s words in his first inaugural still ring true: "In every dark hour of our national life, a leadership of frankness and vigor has met with that understanding and support of the people themselves which is essential to victory."

Roosevelt fulfilled the role of moral leadership. So did Wilson and Lincoln, Truman and Jackson and Teddy Roosevelt. They led the people as well as the Government—they fought for great ideals as well as bills. And the time has come to demand that kind of leadership again.

And so, as this vital campaign begins, let us discuss the issues the next President will face—but let us also discuss the powers and tools with which we must face them.

For we must endow that office with extraordinary strength and vision. We must act in the image of Abraham Lincoln summoning his wartime Cabinet to a meeting on the Emancipation Proclamation. That Cabinet has been carefully chosen to please and reflect many elements in the country. But "I have gathered you together," Lincoln said, "to hear what I have written down. I do not wish your advice about the main matter—that I have determined for myself."

And later, when he went to sign after several hours of exhausting handshaking that had left his arm weak, he said to those present: "If my name goes down in history, it will be for this act. My whole soul is in it. If my hand trembles when I sign this proclamation, all who examine the document hereafter will say: 'He hesitated.'"

But Lincoln's hand did not tremble. He did not hesitate. He did not equivocate.

The Presidency and the Responsibilities of Power

JOHN F. KENNEDY

In a television interview with three correspondents in December, 1962, President Kennedy discussed his views of the office, based upon his experience in the White House. What impressed him, he said, was on the one hand the limitations put upon the President, and on the other, the latitude afforded him to control events. He had also found it more difficult than he thought it would be to obtain from Congress the legislative program desired by his administration. Further, he had found that there was a necessity for constant attention to administration so that policies might be coordinated and implemented.

When a President put his prestige "on the line," as Kennedy did in his skirmish with the steel companies, it was very important, he asserted, that he be reasonably certain of attaining his objective.

Public Papers of the Presidents of the United States, John F. Kennedy, 1962 (Washington, D.C.: U.S. Government Printing Office, 1963), pp. 889-904.

The responsibility of the President in a nuclear age was awesome, he said, for the consequences of erroneous judgment or imprudent action were too terrible to contemplate.

These remarks should be read as a supplement to Kennedy's foregoing statement made during his candidacy, for together they reveal the gap between theory and practice.

WILLIAM H. LAWRENCE (AMERICAN BROADCASTING COMPANY): As you look back upon your first two years in office, sir, has your experience in the office matched your expectations? You had studied a good deal the power of the Presidency, the methods of its operations. How has this worked out as you saw it in advance?

THE PRESIDENT: Well, I think in the first place the problems are more difficult than I had imagined they were. Secondly, there is a limitation upon the ability of the United States to solve these problems. We are involved now in the Congo in a very difficult situation. We have been unable to secure an implementation of the policy which we have supported. We are involved in a good many other areas. We are trying to see if a solution can be found to the struggle between Pakistan and India, with whom we want to maintain friendly relations. Yet they are unable to come to an agreement. There is a limitation, in other words, upon the power of the United States to bring about solutions.

I think our people get awfully impatient and maybe fatigued and tired, and saying "We have been carrying this burden for 17 years; can we lay it down?" We can't lay it down, and I don't see how we are going to lay it down in this century.

So that I would say that the problems are more difficult than I had imagined them to be. The responsibilities placed on the United States are greater than I imagined them to be, and there are greater limitations upon our ability to bring about a favorable result than I had imagined them to be. And I think that is probably true of anyone who becomes President, because there is such a difference between those who advise or speak or legislate, and between the man who must select from the various alternatives proposed and say that this shall be the policy of the United States. It is much easier to make the speeches than it is to finally make the judgments, because unfortunately your advisors are frequently divided. If you take the wrong course, and on occasion I have, the President bears the burden of the responsibility quite rightly. The advisors may move on to new advice.

LAWRENCE: Well, Mr. President, that brings up a point that has always interested me. How does a President go about making a decision, like Cuba, for example?

THE PRESIDENT: The most recent one was hammered out really on policy and decision over a period of five or six days. During that period, the 15 people more or less who were directly consulted frequently changed their view, because whatever action we took had so many disadvantages to it, and each action we took raised the prospect that it might escalate with the Soviet Union into a nuclear war. Finally, however, I think a general consensus developed, and certainly seemed after all alternatives were examined that the course of action that we finally adopted was the right one. . . .

GEORGE E. HERMAN (COLUMBIA BROADCASTING SYSTEM): I would like to go back to the question of the consensus and your relationship to the consensus. You have said and the Constitution says that the decision can be made only by the President.

THE PRESIDENT: Well, you know that old story about Abraham Lincoln and the Cabinet. He says, "All in favor, say 'aye'," and the whole cabinet voted "aye," and then "All opposed, no," and Lincoln voted "No," and he said, "The vote is no." So that naturally the Constitution places the responsibility on the President. There was some disagreement with the course we finally adopted, but the course we finally adopted had the advantage of permitting other steps if this one was unsuccessful. In other words, we were starting in a sense at a minimum place. Then if that were unsuccessful, we could have gradually stepped it up until we had gone into a much more massive action, which might have become necessary if the first step had been unsuccessful. I would think that the majority finally came to accept that, though at the beginning there was a much sharper division. And after all, this was very valuable, because the people who were involved had particular responsibilities of their own; Mr. McNamara, Secretary of Defense, therefore had to advise me on the military capacity of the United States in that area, the Secretary of State, who had to advise on the attitude of the OAS and NATO. So that in my opinion, the majority came to accept the course we finally took. It made it much easier. In the Cuba of 1961, the advice of those who were brought in on the Executive Branch was also unanimous, and the advice was wrong. And I was responsible. So that finally it comes down that no matter how many advisers you have, frequently they are divided, and the President must finally choose.

The other point is something that President Eisenhower said to

me on January 19th. He said "There are no easy matters that will ever
come to you as President. If they are easy, they will be settled at a lower
level." So that the matters that come to you as President are always
the difficult matters, and matters that carry with them large implications.
So this contributes to some of the burdens of the office of the Presidency,
which other Presidents have commented on. . . .

LAWRENCE: As a young Congressman, sir, you voted to impose a two-
term limitation on Presidents. Now that you have held the office for a
while, and also observed its effect on President Eisenhower's second term,
would you repeat that vote, even if the amendment did not apply to
yourself?

THE PRESIDENT: Yes, I would. I would. I know the conditions were
special in '47, but I think eight years is enough, and I am not sure that
a President, in my case if I were re-elected, that you are at such a dis-
advantage. There are not many jobs. That is not the power of the Presidency, patronage, at all. They are filled in the first months. Most of those
jobs belong to the members of the Congress, anyway. So patronage is not
a factor. I think there are many other powers of the Presidency that run
in the second term as well as the first.

SANDER VANOCUR (NATIONAL BROADCASTING COMPANY): Mr. President,
on that point—

THE PRESIDENT: The fact of the matter is President Eisenhower has
great influence today in the Republican Party, and therefore in the
country, and has great influence in foreign policy, and he does not even
hold office. In some ways his influence is greater to some degree. So that
the same is really also true of President Truman and President Hoover.
I don't think that it depends—the influence of a President is still substantial in his second term, though I haven't had a second term—I think
it is. . . .

It is a tremendous change to go from being a Senator to being President. In the first months, it is very difficult. But I have no reason to
believe that a President with the powers of this office and the responsibilities placed on it, if he has a judgment that some things need to be
done, I think he can do it just as well the second time as the first, depending, of course, on the make-up of the Congress. The fact is, I think,
the Congress looks more powerful sitting here than it did when I was
there in the Congress. But that is because when you are in the Congress
you are one of a hundred in the Senate or one of 435 in the House. So
that the power is so divided. But from here I look at a Congress, and I

look at the collective power of the Congress, particularly the bloc action, and it is a substantial power.

VANOCUR: Do you think we could turn for a moment to this subject of the President's responsibility in foreign affairs? Now, when some Congressman disagreed with your course of action over Cuba on that Monday, the responsibility you have by the Constitution in this is very clear, but in domestic matters, the responsibility is divided. How do you use the Presidency in Theodore Roosevelt's phrase, "the bully pulpit," to move these men who really are kind of barons and sovereigns in their own right up there on the Hill? Have you any way to move them toward a course of action which you think is imperative?

THE PRESIDENT: Well, the Constitution and the development of the Congress all give advantage to delay. It is very easy to defeat a bill in the Congress. It is much more difficult to pass one. To go through a committee, say the Ways and Means Committee of the House, subcommittee, and get a majority vote, the full committee and get a majority vote, go to the Rules Committee and get a rule, go to the Floor of the House and get a majority, start over again in the Senate, subcommittee and full committee, and in the Senate there is unlimited debate, so you can never bring a matter to a vote if there is enough determination on the part of the opponents, even if they are a minority, to go through the Senate with the bill. And then unanimously get a conference between the House and Senate to adjust the bill, or if one member objects, to have it go back through the Rules Committee, back through the Congress, and have this done on a controversial piece of legislation where powerful groups are opposing it, that is an extremely difficult task. So that the struggle of a President who has a program to move it through the Congress, particularly when the seniority system may place particular individuals in key positions who may be wholly unsympathetic to your program, and may be, even though they are members of your own party, in political opposition to the President, this is a struggle which every President who has tried to get a program through has had to deal with. After all, Franklin Roosevelt was elected by the largest majority in history in 1936, and he got his worst defeat a few months afterwards in the Supreme Court bill.

So that they are two separate offices and two separate powers, the Congress and the Presidency. There is bound to be conflict, but they must cooperate to the degree that is possible. But that is why no President's program is ever put in. The only time a President's program is put in quickly and easily is when the program is insignificant. But if it is significant and affects important interests and is controversial, therefore, then there is a fight, and the President is never wholly successful.

VANOCUR: Mr. President, which is the better part of wisdom, to take a bill which is completely emasculated, that you had great interest in and accept it, or accept its defeat in the hope of building up public support for it at a later time?

THE PRESIDENT: Well, I would say given the conditions you described, I think it would be better to accept the defeat, but usually what has happened, and what has happened to us in the last two years, a good many of our bills passed in reasonable position, not the way we sent them up, but after all, the Congress has its own will and its own feelings and its own judgment, and they are close to the people. The whole House of Representatives has just been elected. So that it is quite natural that they will have a different perspective than I may have. So I would say what we ought to do is to do the best we can. But if it is completely emasculated, then there is no sense in having a shadow of success and not the substance.

LAWRENCE: Mr. President, in the exercise of Presidential power, and I think perhaps the best known case and the most widely talked about was your rollback of steel prices after they had been announced by the steel companies, some people have suggested that in retrospect that perhaps you would not have acted so vigorously. Is there any truth in this suggestion?

THE PRESIDENT: I must say it would have been a very serious situation, though I don't like to rake over old fires, I think it would have been a serious situation if I had not attempted with all my influence to try to get a rollback, because there was an issue of good faith involved. The steel union had accepted the most limited settlement that they had had since the end of the second war, they had accepted it three or four months ahead, they did it in part, I think, because I said that we could not afford another inflationary spiral, that it would affect our competitive position abroad, so they signed up. Then when their last contract was signed, which was the Friday or Saturday before, then steel put its prices up immediately. It seemed to me that the question of good faith was involved, and that if I had not attempted, after asking the unions to accept the non-inflationary settlement, if I had not attempted to use my influence to have the companies hold their prices stable, I think the union could have rightfully felt that they had been misled. In my opinion it would have endangered the whole bargaining between labor and management, would have made it impossible for us to exert any influence from the public point of view in the future on these great labor-management disputes which do affect the public interest. So I have no regrets. The fact is, we were successful.

Now, supposing we had tried and made a speech about it, and then failed. I would have thought that would have been an awful setback to the office of the Presidency. Now, I just think, looking back on it, that I would not change it at all. There is no sense in raising hell, and then not being successful. There is no sense in putting the office of the Presidency on the line on an issue, and then being defeated. Now, an unfortunate repercussion of that was the strong feeling that the government might interfere in a good many labor-management matters, or that it might interfere in the whole question of the free enterprise system. It was regrettable that that general conclusion was drawn in this particular incident. Given the problem that I had on that Tuesday night, I must say I think we had to do everything we could to get it reversed. . . .

LAWRENCE: Mr. President, you spoke the other day of the dangers and difficulties of slow communications between here and the Soviet Union, as it exhibited itself during the Cuban crisis. I suppose this would be an even greater problem if your radar screen were to pick up missiles or at least what appeared to be missiles in any substantial number?

THE PRESIDENT: Yes. Well, there is—one of the arguments for the continuation of the airplane is that if you picked up missiles coming toward you, you could have your planes take off and be in the air. Then if it proved to be a false alarm, then you could call them back. For missiles, you can't do that, and the President might have to make a judgment in a 15-minute period, and the information would be incomplete. You recall that incident where the moon came up, and it appeared to be a whole variety of missiles coming in. Of course, it was picked up several years ago. I think that is oversimplified. The fact of the matter is that the United States could wait quite long because we have missiles in hardened sites, and those missiles, even if there was a missile attack on the United States, those missiles could still be fired and destroy the Soviet Union, and so could the Polaris submarine missiles. So that I don't think there is a danger that we would fire based on incomplete and inaccurate information, because we were only given five or six minutes to make a judgment. I think the Polaris alone permits us to wait to make sure that we are going to have sufficient in hand that he knows that we could destroy the Soviet Union. Actually that is the purpose of the deterrent. Once he fires his missiles, it is all over anyway, because we are going to have sufficient resources to fire back at him to destroy the Soviet Union. When that day comes, and there is a massive exchange, then that is the end, because you are talking about Western Europe, the Soviet Union, the United States, of 150 million fatalities in the first 18 hours. Now, you could go on, if everybody aimed at cities in order to have as many killed as possible in all these communities with all the weapons you could fire, you could kill, and you might be having more fire. So that the nuclear age is a very dangerous period, and that is why I frequently read these speeches about how we must do this and that. But I think they ought to just look at what we are talking about.

LAWRENCE: How urgent is this need for quicker communication between here and the Soviet Union?

THE PRESIDENT: It is desirable. It is not—if he fires his missiles at us, it is not going to do any good for us to have a telephone at the Kremlin but I do think that—and ask him whether it is really true. But I do think it is better that we should be quicker than we now are. It took us some hours in the Cuban matter, and I think that communication is important. In addition to the communications with the Kremlin, we have very poor communications to a good deal of Latin America, and we don't know what is going on there very frequently. So we are trying to improve our communications all around the world, because that knowledge is so vital to an effective decision. . . .

VANOCUR: Mr. President, back before you were elected, your father used to have a favorite story he told reporters. He asked you once why do you want the job, and he cited the reasons why you shouldn't want it, and you apparently gave him an answer—I don't know whether it satisfied him, but apparently you satisfied yourself. Would you give him the same answer today after serving in this office for two years?

THE PRESIDENT: Oh, you mean that somebody is going to do it?

VANOCUR: Yes, sir.

THE PRESIDENT: Yes. I think that there are a lot of satisfactions to the Presidency, particularly, as I say, we are all concerned as citizens and as parents and all the rest, with all the problems we have been talking about tonight. They are all the problems which if I was not the President, I would be concerned about as a father or a citizen. So at least you have an opportunity to do something about them. And if what you do is useful and successful, then of course that is a great satisfaction. When as a result of a decision of yours, failure comes, or you are unsuccessful, then of course that is a great setback. But I must say after being here for two years, and having the experience of the Presidency, and there is no experience you can get that can possibly prepare you adequately for the Presidency, I must say that I have a good deal of hope for the United States. Just because I think that this country, which, as I say, criticizes itself and is criticized around the world, 180 million people, for 17 years, really for more than that, for almost 20 years, have been the great means of defending first the world against the Nazi threat, and since then against the Communist threat, and if it were not for us, the Communists would be dominant in the world today, and because of us, we are in a strong position. Now, I think that is a pretty good record for a country with 6 per cent of the world's population, which is very reluctant to take on these burdens. I think we ought to be rather pleased with ourselves this Christmas.

7

Lyndon B. Johnson Discusses the Presidency

Seven times in the nation's history, Presidents have died in office or been assassinated, but always the transition of power has been peaceful, a tribute to the viability of the American constitutional system. One immediate concern after such a tragedy has been to maintain the confidence of the people in their government, and, in the modern era, to reassure the world of the continuity of American foreign policy.

In the following excerpts from a television interview, President Johnson relates how he handled the problem of sudden transition. He also expresses his views on the responsibilities of presidential leadership, declaring that party leadership in the traditional sense should be supplemented by "consensus" politics, and that the Chief Executive can truly be "President of all the people."

WILLIAM H. LAWRENCE (AMERICAN BROADCASTING COMPANY): Mr. President, considering the violent and abrupt manner of your succession to the Presidency, I think everyone agrees that the transition has gone remarkably smoothly. Did this just happen, or did you start to plan these things, say, in those few hours in Air Force 1 as you flew back from Dallas?

Department of State Bulletin (*April 6, 1964*), pp. 523-524, 529.

THE PRESIDENT: Well, we had a lot of help in the planning, Mr. Lawrence. A lot of thoughts that went through my mind, as I left the hospital, and on the way to Air Force 1, and while we were waiting for Judge Hughes and Mrs. Kennedy to come aboard—I wasn't sure whether this was an international conspiracy, or just what it was, or what might happen next. I was sure that the whole Nation had been shaken and the world would be in doubt.

As I rode back, I recognized that our first great problem was to assure the world that there would be continuity in transition, that our constitutional system would work. I realized the importance of uniting our people at home and asking them to carry forward with the program; so I immediately planned to have the bipartisan leaders come to the White House upon my arrival.

I asked the members of the Cabinet who were then in town, the Director of the National Security Council, and Mr. McNamara and others to meet me at Andrews, and I appealed to all of those men to work with me on the transition and to try to so conduct ourselves as to assure the rest of the world that we did have continuity and assure the people of this country that we expected them to unite.

Very shortly thereafter, President Eisenhower came down and spent some time with me exploring the problems that he expected to arise confronting a new President. President Truman came in and gave me his counsel, and we started off with the help and plans of a good many people and substantially well organized.

I don't know how well the Government did its part of the transition, but the people's part was well done.

MR. LAWRENCE: What were your first priorities, Mr. President?

THE PRESIDENT: The first priority was to try to display to the world that we could have continuity and transition, that the program of President Kennedy would be carried on, that there was no need for them to be disturbed and fearful that our constitutional system had been endangered—to demonstrate to the people of this country that, although their leader had fallen and we had a new President, we must have unity and we must close ranks and we must work together for the good of all America and the world.

MR. LAWRENCE: Well, did you have any concern about the international posture that you must adopt so that, one, all of our allies would be reassured, and our potential enemies wouldn't get any wrong ideas?

THE PRESIDENT: Oh, yes; and I spent the first full week meeting with more than 90 representatives from the nations of the world and trying to explain to them our constitutional system, and what they could expect under it, and how we carry on the program that we had begun, and that I had been a part of the Kennedy-Johnson ticket that won the election in 1960, that we had a Kennedy-Johnson program, that I had been a participant in the formulation of that program, and that we would carry it on—maybe not as well as the late President could have, had he lived, but as best we could—and they need have no fear or no doubt. . . .

MR. LAWRENCE: Mr. President, you have now been President for something over 100 days. You have been around Washington for more than 30 years. How is the view from the inside as compared with the view from the outside?

THE PRESIDENT: Well, it is a much tougher job from the inside than I thought it was from the outside.

I have watched it since Mr. Hoover's days, and I realized the responsibilities it carried, and the obligations of leadership that were there, and the decisions that had to be made, and the awesome responsibilities of the office.

But I must say that, when I started having to make those decisions and started hearing from the Congress, the Presidency looked a little different when you are in the Presidency than it did when you are in the Congress, and vice versa.

MR. LAWRENCE: Mr. President, Thomas Jefferson referred to the office as a splendid misery. Harry Truman used to talk about it as if it were a prison cell. Do you like it?

THE PRESIDENT: I am doing the best I can in it, and I am enjoying what I am doing.

Thomas Jefferson said the second office of the land was an honorable and easy one. The Presidency was a splendid misery. But I found great interest in serving in both offices, and it carries terrific and tremendous and awesome responsibilities, but I am proud of this nation and I am so grateful that I could have an opportunity that I have had in America that I want to give my life seeing that the opportunity is perpetuated for others.

I am so proud of our system of government, of our free enterprise, where our incentive system and our men who head our big industries are willing to get up at daylight and get to bed at midnight to offer employment and create new jobs for people, where our men working there will try to get decent wages but will sit across the table and not act like cannibals, but will negotiate and reason things out together.

I am so happy to be a part of a system where the average per capita income is in excess of $200 per month, when there are only six nations in the entire world that have as much as $80 per month, and while the Soviet Union has three times as many tillable acres of land as we have and a population that's in excess of ours and a great many resources that we don't have, that if properly developed would exceed our potential in water and oil and so forth, nevertheless we have one thing they don't have and that is our system of private enterprise, free enterprise, where the employer, hoping to make a little profit, the laborer, hoping to justify his wages, can get together and make a better mousetrap.

They have developed this into the most powerful and leading nation in the world, and I want to see it preserved. And I have an opportunity to do something about it as President.

And I may not be a great President, but as long as I am here, I am going to try to be a good President and do my dead-level best to see this system preserved, because when the final chips are down it is not going to be the number of people we have or the number of acres or the number of resources that win; the thing that is going to make us win is our system of government.

DAVID BRINKLEY (NATIONAL BROADCASTING COMPANY): Thank you, Mr. President.

part three

▪▪▪▪▪▪▪▪▪▪▪▪▪▪▪▪▪▪▪▪▪▪▪

PERSPECTIVES ON THE PRESIDENCY

I

The Powers of the Contemporary President

ROBERT S. HIRSCHFIELD

During the early years of the Republic, the Presidents were men of exceptional ability and stature. Their reputations and the popular esteem in which they were held endowed the office with a prestige which it might not otherwise have acquired. In the long period (1833-1901) between the administrations of Andrew Jackson and Theodore Roosevelt, however, with but one outstanding exception, a succession of mediocrities occupied the White House. Congress filled the vacuum and thus became the center of leadership until the circumstances of twentieth-century life shifted the balance.

In the forseeable future, the President's position at the center of national affairs will remain unchallenged for three vital reasons: (1) the continuing American involvement in "limited" wars; (2) the continuing political and economic competition with the Soviet Union; and (3) the necessity to extend social and economic democracy at home. Although the President's power is subject to restraint by the courts, the legislature, and public opinion, none of these external forces can seriously hobble him if he chooses to exercise his role as the popular leader who reflects the popular aspirations of the country. The following selection clearly summarizes the new dimensions of Presidential leadership.

IN GENERAL TERMS the Presidency at the beginning of the 1960's is easily described: It is the focus of both the American governmental system and the free world coalition, an office of great authority and commensurate responsibility. Resting firmly on the twin supports of democratic election and the necessities of a critical era, it is now a permanently strong office, an institutionalized version of the "crisis presidencies" of Lincoln, Wilson, Roosevelt, and Truman. And like the regimes from which it stems, the outstanding feature of the executive office today is its power.

* * *

Robert S. Hirschfield, "The Power of the Contemporary Presidency," Parliamentary Affairs, *XIV (Summer, 1961), 353-377. Reprinted by permission of The Hansard Society for Parliamentary Government and the author.*

THE SOURCES OF PRESIDENTIAL POWER

Although theoretically the twin fountainheads of executive power are the "Constitution and the laws," in fact the sources of this prodigious authority are now democracy and necessity.

The Presidency, like all offices of government, is only a paper institution until the political process supplies the personality which brings it to life. And Article II, though it outlines a potentially powerful executive office, has no effect until its words are translated into action. The real foundations of presidential power, therefore, are those forces which elevate the executive to a focal position in government, allowing him to interpret his authority broadly and to exercise it boldly.

The most important of these forces lies in the democratic nature of the modern Presidency. Not only constitutionally, but also politically and psychologically, the President is *the* leader of the nation. "His," as Woodrow Wilson said, "is the only national voice in affairs. Let him once win the admiration and confidence of the country, and no other single force can withstand him, no combination of forces will easily overpower him. His position takes the imagination of the country. He is the representative of no constituency, but of the whole people." Whether the explanation for the unique popular response to the Presidency be put in politico-constitutional terms (the election process and the singular form of the office) or in psycho-sociological terms (the desire for a father-image and the need for a symbol of national unity), the fact remains that its power flows from and is primarily dependent on its tribunate character.

The personality and political philosophy of the President are closely related to his democratic leadership. All of our strongest Presidents have had charismatic personalities, and all have been power-oriented in their philosophy of government, for it is the combination of popular attraction to the person and popular support for his political principles which makes the President's power effective. Thus his role as Popular Tribune is basic to the exercise of whatever authority may be latent in the Constitution and the laws. Neither Lincoln nor Roosevelt could have acted with such spectacular independence in meeting the challenges that confronted them had they lacked solid popular support, but with that support, they could push their powers to the limits of constitutionality and beyond. Indeed a number of strong Presidents have received object lessons regarding the dependence of power upon popular support: Truman in the 1952 steel dispute, Wilson during the League fight,

Roosevelt when he presented the Court-packing plan, and Lincoln's successor after the Civil War's end. Extending one of Woodrow Wilson's observations, the President can dominate American government (Wilson said "his party") by being "spokesman for the real sentiment and purpose of the country, by giving direction to opinion, by giving the country at once the information and the statements of policy which will enable it to form its judgments alike of parties and of men."

All strong Presidents have recognized the importance of maintaining a close relationship with their major source of power. Jackson's election, heralding the era of mass democracy, established the popular Presidency, and Lincoln made clear its significance under crisis conditions. Wilson, following the lead of Theodore Roosevelt, gave the conception further impetus by his practice of "going to the people" on important issues. And Franklin Roosevelt, through masterful use of modern communications media, brought the tribunate Presidency to its contemporary form. Radio, television and the press conference have made possible the development of a relationship between the President and the people which is exceedingly close. As a result of this intimate —almost familial—bond, the President's constitutional role as symbol of national unity has become an instrument of tremendous power, making him the centre of our governmental system, and creating the basis for his leadership both at home and abroad.

The other, and no less important, source of presidential power is necessity. Not only the psychological need for clearly identifiable and deeply trusted authority, but also the governmental necessity for centralized leadership and decisive action in times of crisis.

Ours is a system constitutionally attuned to the requirements of the eighteenth century, and it is mainly through the development of the Presidency that the system has been adapted to the demands of the twentieth. The separation of powers, federalism, even the Bill of Rights and the rule of law, must sometimes be transcended under conditions of grave national emergency. Even under less pressing circumstances, the need for purposeful and efficient government is increasingly evident. But the legislative process—complex, deliberative, cumbersome, and designed to assure the compromise of manifold local interests—is illsuited to meet these challenges. Only the President, possessing (as Alexander Hamilton noted) both unity and energy, can meet the demand for leadership under critical conditions.

Again, every strong President has recognized this fact and acted in accordance with it. Lincoln arrogated to himself all the powers of government during his eleven-week "dictatorship" in 1861 on the ground that "whether strictly legal or not" his actions were ventured upon "under what appeared to be a popular demand and a public necessity." In the atmosphere of world war, Congress accepted Wilson's leadership and delegated theretofore unprecedented power to the President. Similarly, it was the pressure of economic catastrophe which elevated FDR to the dominant position he occupied during the first hundred days of the New Deal administration, and the existence of an even greater emergency which made him supreme commander of the nation during the Second World War. Likewise, Truman's warmaking power sprang from the need for decisive action to halt aggression. Necessity creates power, and presidential power has always been commensurate with the nation's needs.

Most significant for our time, however, is the fact—clearly demonstrated by the Korean conflict and other events since the end of World War II—that the Communist challenge has created a permanent demand for strong leadership and extraordinary power. Because crisis has become the normal condition of our times, the vast authority available to former Presidents only occasionally has today become a permanent part of the executive office.

Thus the needs of the nation and the support of its citizens are the real sources of presidential power, unlocking all the authority hidden in the Constitution and the laws, as well as availing the executive of powers which go beyond even the broadest interpretation of that prodigious combination. The modern President can draw upon extraordinary power because he is the democratic symbol of national unity and the necessary instrument of national action, because it is to him that the nation turns for crisis leadership and because he alone can supply that leadership. As a result, under critical conditions there are no effective constitutional or governmental limits on executive power, for democracy and necessity allow the President to transcend the limitational principle and assert his full authority as trustee of the nation's destiny.

THE RESTRAINTS ON PRESIDENTIAL POWER

In our society there are ostensibly many restraints on presidential power. The federal system, for example, establishes fifty centres of local authority to contend with the national executive. The nation's socioeconomic "power elite" represents another potential element of countervailing force. Even within the executive branch itself there is the kind of restraint which flows from administrative inertia or obstruction. But whatever limitations appear to reside in these areas, basically there are three major forms of external restraint on presidential power: judicial supervision, legislative control, and public opinion.

Judicial restraint. Of these the least effective—despite its vaunted reputation—is judicial review of executive acts. And the basic reason is clear: in a showdown the President's power is greater than the Supreme Court's. The judicial branch has generally recognized this fact and either avoided conflict with the executive when possible or accepted his assertions of authority when forced to reach a decision. Indeed the Court has established a consistent pattern of acquiescence in judging presidential exercises of extraordinary power. This acquiescent attitude is not automatic, but in only one instance of direct conflict between the two branches during an emergency period has an important exercise of independent presidential authority been effectively overturned, and then the actual holding was so narrow as to have little permanent value. It is the lesson of history that where exercises of extraordinary power are involved, the Court restrains itself and not the President.

* * *

The judiciary is always placed in a difficult position by conditions which allow a strong President to assume extraordinary power. Compelled to acknowledge that the law of necessity is superior to the law of the Constitution, and lacking the kind of popular support which is accorded the political leader, it must accept many actions which under normal conditions would be outside the realm of legitimate power. The Court's infrequent *ex post facto* pronouncements regarding the limits of presidential authority have little direct effect in any case, and since no judicial decision is self-enforcing they are always essentially lectures rather than injunctions. The Court's primary function in checking a strong President is to act as a symbol of restraint, a moral force and a constant reminder of established principles—a function which is by no means unimportant—but with regard to executive power, Article II of the Constitution is what the President, and not what the Court, says it is.

Legislative restraint. In our governmental system Congress is traditionally viewed as the President's principal antagonist and most effective restrainer. The constitutional separation of powers with its mechanism of checks and balances was designed to encourage an executive-legislative power struggle which would prevent either branch from gaining dominant authority. And the local orientation of congressional politics supposedly provides a counterweight to the national purview of the Presidency. But despite all this, Congress cannot easily control the exercise of presidential power. Indeed both the constitutional structure of the government, with its separation of the branches, and the nature of American politics, with its emphasis on local interest representation, often tend to make that task more rather than less difficult.

The separation of powers doctrine can become both a shield and a sword in the hands of a strong President. He can use it to ward off alleged congressional encroachments on executive authority, as Lincoln did in combating the Committee on the Conduct of the (Civil) War and as Wilson did in preventing the establishment of a similar body. Or he can use the doctrine to support his resort to independent authority, the approach adopted on so many occasions by the Civil War President (who achieved the greatest concentration of power in our history by insisting on the separation principle), as well as by every other strong executive who has relied on the principle in assuming extraordinary power on his own initiative.

As the separation of powers principle often creates a constitutional power vacuum which the executive can fill, so too does the nature of congressional politics give rise to conditions which may enhance rather than limit presidential authority. The local orientation of Congress assures the representation of all the significant interests in our society, but at the same time it results in legislative fragmentation, leaving Congress without a cohesive majority or effective leadership. And this political power vacuum the President may also enter. Indeed it is increasingly evident that if he does not assume the role of legislative leader, Congress cannot move on important and controversial issues. Attuned to the process of continuing compromise rather than to the achievement of definite goals, Congress must always give way to the executive when events demand unity of purpose and decisive action.

Congress itself knows this and looks increasingly to the President for leadership, not only with regard to matters of national defence and foreign affairs, but in other areas as well, like domestic economic policy and civil rights. It is in time of actual or impending emergency, however, that this need for presidential initiative is most clearly evident and most readily acknowledged by Congress, as it quickly accepts the President's direction in delegating to him whatever authority he requests. Despite the separation of powers principle, executive leadership of the legislature has become an established feature of our system, though the effect of Congress's reliance on presidential initiative and of its delegations of authority to the executive is to enhance his domination over the legislative process and to increase his freedom from legislative control.

Congress's difficulty in restraining presidential power is also a result of the tremendous range and complexity of contemporary governmental problems, and of its own inability to deal with them. Neither the individual legislator nor the Congress as a whole possesses the information-gathering and problem-evaluating apparatus of the Presidency, particularly in the foreign affairs and defence areas, but in others as well. Congress is increasingly dependent, therefore, upon members of the executive branch—department heads, military officers, economic and scientific advisers—for the technical information essential to its own activity. Thus, while information may be acquired through congressional inquiry or investigation (and despite the fact that the President's subordinates do not always accept his policy determinations), to a large extent the effectiveness of legislative supervision depends upon the executive's willingness to co-operate.

Further detracting from the legislature's ability to contend with the President is his control over formulation of the budget, since this function gives the executive a dominant position in determining the final plan for governmental expenditures. Indeed the congressional power over the executive traditionally assumed to be the greatest—the power of the purse—is often ineffectual. The President may present Congress with a situation which does not permit the withholding of funds, as Theodore Roosevelt did by sending the Great White Fleet on its famous global journey without enough coal to get it back home, and as other Presidents have done by more serious dispositions of the armed forces. Congress may even be forced to appropriate money without knowing the reason for the expenditure, as it did in supporting the secret, multi-billion dollar development of the atomic bomb. And Lincoln simply paid out $3,000,000 of public funds on his own initiative. Despite its celebrated reputation, therefore, even the restraining power of the purse is subject to suspension when the need for secrecy or speed is of the essence.

The most important limitation on Congress as a presidential restrainer, however, is public support for the executive. While the localism of congressional politics makes legislators peculiarly responsive to the desires of particular groups, it also leaves the advantage increasingly with the President in mobilizing the general public behind national policies. For with regard to such policies Congress can never present a single view or project a definite image to the country, while the President can do so forcefully. Emphasizing his roles as head of state and sole national representative, and utilizing all the media of mass communication, he is able to generate pressure which Congress cannot easily withstand.

Of course Congress is not impotent in exercising control over the President. The political longevity of congressional leaders and the absence of party discipline allow for displays of legislative independence which can and do embarrass or inhibit the executive. Legislative debate and investigation—techniques which have been used to harass every strong President—can focus attention on alleged maladministration or misconduct in the executive branch. And widespread congressional hostility makes even the strongest President somewhat cautious in his exercises of power. But under emergency or semi-emergency conditions congressional antagonism is largely sublimated, and attempts to limit the President are generally more irritating than effective. Despite legislative fulmination, no crisis executive has ever been deterred by the legislature from accomplishing his major purposes.

Indeed, confronted with a strong President, Congress generally finds the task of imposing restraints both thankless and frustrating. For the public is likely to equate opposition to the President with obstruction of his efforts in the nation's behalf, and moreover there is the hard fact that a popular crisis President who encounters difficulties or delays in Congress—particularly in matters of foreign policy—may simply by-pass the legislature and present it with a *fait accompli* by resort to his independent authority. Congress is certainly a more formidable check on presidential power than the courts, but in our time it does not and cannot fulfil the restraining function traditionally ascribed to it.

Popular restraint. As the President's principal source of power is public support, so too can popular opinion be the most important restraint on that power. So long as the nation's approval is firm and evident, his authority cannot be challenged effectively, but conversely, in order to use his full powers a President must continue to have such approval. His personal relationship with the public and his ability to guide popular opinion are the mainstays of his dominant position in government.

* * *

The major instrumentalities for mobilizing public support against the President are the opposition political party, organized pressure groups, and the press or other communications media. But under critical conditions particularly, the same factors that limit the efficacy of the formal (legislative and judicial) restraints also apply to these three informal restraining forces. The President's political opponents—often including members of his own party—must beware of boomerangs; pressure groups represent only single rather than national interests; and the media, perhaps the most important of the three, fear that by combining their reportorial and editorial functions in opposing the President, they may lose the public trust, limit their wide area of freedom, and cut off their best sources of news. The press, radio, and television report and comment on opposition to the executive, but even when the diverse elements of the communications system agree with this opposition, they seldom attempt to incite public disapproval of his actions.

While popular support may, on rare occasions, be mobilized against the President, the opposite is the rule. For he is the principal moulder of popular opinion, and as a result, even this most important instrument of restraint is not often effective. The same psychology that creates a desire for presidential leadership in critical times assures the executive of popular support for the policies which he pursues. Moreover, it is important to recognize that this "crisis psychology" which elevates the President to a dominant position is itself partly created by the President. For, given the framework of objective facts surrounding a critical situation, it is largely the crisis leader's own reaction to those facts—the extent to which he emphasizes and dramatizes the situation's seriousness —that determines the form of public response.

* * *

Whatever the objective facts may be, it is the President himself who plays a central role in defining the issues and creating the popular attitudes which make possible his own exercises of extraordinary power. Moreover, all of this is especially true in our own time, not only because the means by which the President may influence opinion have improved so greatly, nor because his ability to use those means is so far superior to that of any other person or group in the society, but because even that segment of the public which is not politically indifferent finds it increasingly difficult to make independent judgments regarding the significance or seriousness of particular events.

* * *

Confronted with fantastically complex problems and asked to determine the wisdom of policies involving all the areas of the world, even the responsible and informed citizen often ends up placing his trust in God and the President. In the sense of its direct influence on decision-making, therefore, public opinion is less a limitation on presidential power than the key to its full utilization—a fact which every strong President has recognized by placing the greatest emphasis on his position of popular leadership.

But if public opinion is ultimately no more effective than legislative or judicial restraint, are there no real limitations on the Presidency? There does exist in our political system one factor which can generally be counted on to minimize the possibility of arbitrary executive rule, and that is the process by which the President is selected. Not merely the element of choice in voting, though that is important, but rather the complex procedure by which candidates are selected in party conventions, and even more, the personal attributes of those who are finally chosen to seek the highest office.

Because the Presidency (along with the Vice-Presidency) is the only national elective office in an exceedingly diverse society, it is open only to those who are attuned to the virtues of political compromise and moderate in their political philosophy. The parties will nominate only such men, and though this tends to exclude from consideration many competent people whose views are too definite, it also acts as a "safety valve" against those who might disregard the welfare of significant segments of our population. A new President may reveal or find within himself the capacity for bold and decisive leadership, but the basic personality, shaped by the same forces that open the way to the office, remains, and even in his assertions of extraordinary power he will not depart essentially from the conservative, evolutionary, and pragmatic tradition of American government and politics.

The Presidency reflects this tradition with remarkable accuracy in its consistent rejection of dogmatism, of the Left and of the Right alike. It is not a position for radical or reactionary autocrats, or for demagogues, and none of our strong Presidents, despite their claims to power, has given any evidence of desiring to establish a permanent dictatorship. Nor has any of them ever attempted to use temporary powers to achieve fundamentally different forms of social or political organization. Some Presidents have assumed dictatorial authority to meet crises, but none has ever *been* a dictator. In power they may sometimes violate basic principles of the constitutional system temporarily, even unnecessarily—as Wilson did by allowing over-zealous subordinates to engage in witchhunting during World War I, and as Roosevelt did in permitting the denial of basic rights to a racial minority during World War II—but in the final analysis all have displayed a deep attachment to, and a high regard for, those principles.

It is at least partly because of their personal commitment to constitutional democratic processes that crisis Presidents have always attempted to justify their extraordinary actions by reference to the basic law, and that whenever possible they have sought to include Congress as a partner in crisis government. For legitimacy is important to the President, as it is to the Presidency, and presidential self-restraint, reflecting both innate personal qualities and real concern for the opinion of the public and of history, can be as meaningful a restraining force as countervailing power. Thus, while constitutional and political methods of restraining the executive may not always be effective, the Presidency has auto-limitational features which tend to mitigate those dangers to our system of government which are inherent in its vast power.

THE PRESIDENCY IN THE '60s

The scope and effect of executive power are today so broad as to make valid Henry Jones Ford's observation that in the presidential office American democracy has revived "the oldest political institution of the race, the elective kingship." Indeed considering the absence of external restraints on this power, the question arises as to whether the contemporary Presidency is not, potentially, a "matrix for dictatorship."

The answer is certainly "no" if by dictatorship is meant absolute and arbitrary authority which denies the opportunity for political opposition and rejects the possibility of free, non-political activity. But it is just as clear that the Presidency today is unquestionably the dominant organ of American government, an office permanently and inherently strong, reflecting the institutionalization of crisis concepts established by precedent, legitimized by public acceptance, and sustained by the abnormality of international affairs.

The Presidency has always mirrored the facts of our national life, and under present conditions there is no alternative to a strong executive. Because ours is an age of crisis, it is an age of executive government, and this political truth applies no less surely to the United States than it does to virtually every other country in the world. The powerful American Presidency is part of a global pattern—as evident in the West as in the East—characterized by the expansion and centralization of governmental authority; it is a modern form of a more primitive kind of rule, developed to meet extraordinary challenges and perpetuated while the search for peaceful normalcy continues.

Despite its present eminence, however, the Presidency during the decade ahead will most likely become an even more powerful institution. And not only in the event of war, nor only in the field of foreign affairs. For the '60s will be a critical period, both at home and abroad, even in the absence of armed conflict, and executive authority may have to be exercised in new ways to meet new challenges. Indeed, to a significant degree the outcome of the struggle between Communism and democracy, as well as the resolution of important domestic issues, will depend on the actions of the President. "Without leadership alert and sensitive to change," as Franklin Roosevelt said, "we are bogged up or lose our way," and in our rapidly changing world there is a pressing need for such leadership on both the national and the international scenes.

There are many new ways in which the power of the Presidency may have to be exercised during the decade ahead. Should the ultimate crisis of thermonuclear war occur, the President would necessarily have to assume dictatorial authority over every aspect of whatever remained of our national existence. His power would be total, to meet the totality of the disaster, and the regimes of Lincoln, Wilson, and Roosevelt would seem pale in comparison. But aside from the dread possibility of an atomic emergency, there will probably be at least three major problems in the '60s requiring strong executive action: the occurrence or threat of limited war in various parts of the globe, increasing political and economic competition with the Soviet camp, and the perfection of democracy within the United States itself.

With regard to the problem of limited armed conflict, Mr. Truman broke new ground in the exercise of presidential power when he committed the nation—and its allies—to a major war in Korea entirely on his own initiative, and a future President might well have to act with similar boldness in defence of the national interest. Indeed, the President's responsibility is no longer limited to the maintenance of American security; it now embraces the security of all the free nations. Nor is his new role limited to sporadic instances of military aggression; because of the more subtle threat of Communist political, social, and economic competition, it is a permanent position. In a very real sense, the American President has become the executive of the entire Western

Coalition, and the major instrument for assuring peace and order throughout the world.

To play this expanded executive role will require that the President lead in the formulation of common Western policy and that he assume the task of articulating the basic principles on which the Western Coalition is established. In the struggle for the nations of Asia and Africa, his will be the crucial job of presenting the case for democracy and of capturing the imagination of the uncommitted peoples. This job really starts at home, for the President must first create a climate of public opinion which will support a bold programme of international leadership. To meet the challenge of Communist competition will require an effort much greater than that which was made to save Western Europe from collapse after World War II, but it will require a similar sense of urgency and a similar kind of vision and vitality in the executive office.

The major domestic problem which the President will have to meet in the '60s is related to the achievement of our foreign policy goals, since he cannot be an effective spokesman for democracy abroad so long as equality in civil rights is denied to coloured citizens within the United States. The law of the Constitution is now clear with regard to this matter, but only the President has the prestige and the power to help make that law meaningful. The civil rights issue is not regional but national, and its resolution will depend largely on presidential initiative in mobilizing national sentiment behind the responsible leaders of both races.

In these new and as yet largely unexplored areas of presidential activity lies much of the future development of executive power. The precise form which that development may take cannot be foretold, but its general direction during the years immediately ahead seems clear. For the new President has already expressed an intention to act in the tradition of his "strong" predecessors, viewing his authority broadly and exercising it boldly. Thus he has recognized that the power of the contemporary Presidency is the nation's principal weapon for meeting the extraordinary challenges which now confront it. And though a President's determination to provide effective leadership cannot alone decide the nation's destiny, it nonetheless constitutes our best hope that those challenges will be met successfully.

2

The Presidency Is No Place for Amateurs

RICHARD NEUSTADT

If the President is to exercise effective leadership, he must be adept in the uses of power. He must be skilled in exerting personal influence and possess expertise in governmental affairs. He must have a sense of purpose that will inspire others to have confidence in him so that he can balance his numerous constituencies at home and abroad. In Professor Neustadt's opinion, only an extraordinary politician—adroit, insightful, and intuitive—can be a successful Chief Executive.

. . . . GOVERNMENTAL POWER, in reality not form, is influence of an effective sort on the behavior of men actually involved in making public policy and carrying it out. Effective influence for the man in the White House stems from three related sources: first are the bargaining advantages inherent in his job with which to persuade other men that what he wants of them is what their own responsibilities require them to do. Second are the expectations of those other men regarding his ability and will to use the various advantages they think he has. Third are those men's estimates of how his public views him and of how their publics may view them if they do what he wants. In short, his power is the product of his vantage points in government, together with his reputation in the Washington community and his prestige outside.

A President, himself, affects the flow of power from these sources, though whether they flow freely or run dry he never will decide alone. He makes his personal impact by the things he says and does. Accordingly, his choices of what he should say and do, and how and when, are his means to conserve and tap the sources of his power. Alternatively, choices are the means by which he dissipates his power. The outcome, case by case, will often turn on whether he perceives his risk in power terms and takes account of what he sees before he makes his choice. A President is so uniquely situated and his power so bound up with the uniqueness of his place, that he can count on no one else to be per-

Richard E. Neustadt, Presidential Power: The Politics of Leadership *(New York, N.Y.: John Wiley & Sons, Inc., 1960), pp. 181-185. Copyright 1960 by John Wiley & Sons, Inc. Reprinted by permission.*

ceptive for him. Yet he can scarcely see and weigh his power stakes himself unless he is alerted by significant details and deals with his decisions in good time. Useful information, timely choices may not reach him; he must do the reaching. To do so is to help himself enhance his personal influence. This is the sort of help he needs the most. But he will neither feel that need nor fill it if his image of his office keeps him faced away from power.

It is natural that Franklin Roosevelt, hungry for the Presidency's power as his birthright, should exemplify the man who helps himself. It is ironic that a Truman, who felt no such hunger and laid claim to no such birthright, still created from his background, and his heroes, and his reading, an image of the office that impelled him toward self-help. It is an equal irony that Eisenhower, hailed by commentators and by voters (and by many intellectuals) as quite uniquely qualified for power in the Presidency, was turned away from self-help by his very qualifications. Only an extraordinary politician could have managed to exploit the opportunities for influence created by the presence of a hero in the White House. But had Eisenhower been a man of politics he never would have come there as the hero that he was. And being what he was, he looked upon his presence there through the eyes of an *anti*-politician. There can be little doubt that he exchanged his hero's welcome for much less than its full value in the currency of power. But how could Eisenhower have done otherwise? His image of himself in office dictated the terms of that exchange.

One never can be sure that when a man becomes the President of the United States his sense of power and of purpose and his own source of self-confidence will show him how to help himself enhance his personal influence. But there is every reason to believe that he will be shown nothing of the sort if he has made the White House his first venture into politics. The Presidency is no place for amateurs.

To make the most of power for himself a President must know what it is made of. This book has treated power in the sense of personal influence and influence in the sense of effectiveness *prospectively,* looking toward tomorrow from today. That look conveys the essence of the task before a man who seeks to maximize his power. If he wants it for the future, he must guard it in the present. He mounts guard, as best he can when he appraises the effects of present action on the sources of his influence. In making that appraisal he has no one to depend on but himself; his power and its sources are a sphere of expertise reserved to him. But the issues that present themselves for action day by day rarely show his personal risks upon their surface. His expertise must first help him to see beneath the surface if it is to help him weigh what may be there. The President as expert does himself a double service. Without the expertise he cannot do it.

The Presidency, to repeat, is not a place for amateurs. That sort of expertise can hardly be acquired without deep experience in political office. The Presidency is a place for men of politics. But by no means is it a place for every politician.

There is no reason to suppose that politicians, on the average, have the wherewithal to help themselves build *presidential* power. The men of politics who specialize in organization work and party office scarcely qualify at all; governmental office is the relevant experience. For present purposes we can regard as politicians only those who build careers in public office. Yet expertise in presidential power does not follow automatically from such experience. No post in government at any level necessarily equips a man to recognize the Presidency's peculiar sources of influence. Those sources have as many parts as a President has constituencies, foreign and domestic; the posts that furnish insights into one part often obscure others. Besides, past officeholding is no guarantee that any man brings with him to the White House the degree and kind of feeling for direction that can help him once he gets there. Former Commerce Secretary Hoover had a sense of purpose so precise as to be stultifying. Former Senator Harding seems to have had none at all. And mere experience, however relevant, is no assurance that a President will find the confidence he needs just when he needs it most. Such confidence requires that his image of himself in office justify an unremitting search for personal power. But it requires, also, that his image of himself allow for failures and frustration in the search. F.D.R. is said to have remarked that Lincoln "was a sad man because he couldn't get it all at once. And nobody can." If a President is to assist himself through the vicissitudes of four long years or eight, his source of confidence must make him capable of bearing Lincoln's sadness with good grace. The power-seeker whose self-confidence requires quick returns and sure success might make a mess of everything including his own power. Grace calls for humor and perspective. Political experience does not assure those qualities. Indeed, it may diminish them in the degree it brings a taste for power. The officeholder who combines them with an insight into presidential influence and hunger for it is no average politician.

Expertise in presidential power seems to be the province not of politicians as a class but of extraordinary politicians. What sets such men apart? Mr. Justice Holmes once characterized Franklin Roosevelt as a "second-rate intellect but a first-rate temperament." Perhaps this is a necessary combination. The politics of well-established government has rarely been attractive to and rarely has dealt kindly with the men whom intellectuals regard as first-rate intellects. Temperament, at any rate, is the great separator. Experience will leave its mark on expertise; so will a man's ambitions for himself and his constituents. But something like that "first-rate" temperament is what turns know-how and desire to his personal account. The necessary confidence is nourished by that temperament. It is a human resource not discovered every day among American politicians.

II

If expertness in maximizing power for himself served purposes no larger than the man's own pride or pleasure, there would be no reason for the rest of us to care whether he were powerful or not. More precisely, there would be no reason except sentiment and partisanship. But a President's success in that endeavor serves objectives far beyond his own and far beyond his party's. For reasons I will come to in a moment. an expert search for presidential influence contributes to the energy of government and to the viability of public policy. Government is energized by a productive tension among its working parts. Policy is kept alive by a sustained transformation of intent into result. Energetic government and viable public policy are at a premium as we begin the seventh decade of the twentieth century. Expertise in presidential power adds to both. A President's constituents, regardless of their party (or their country for that matter), have a great stake in his search for personal influence.

In the American political system the President sits in a unique seat and works within a unique frame of reference. The things he personally has to do are no respecters of the lines between "civil" and "military," or "foreign" and "domestic," or "legislative" and "executive," or "administrative" and "political." At his desk—and there alone—distinctions of these sorts lose their last shred of meaning. The expectations centered in his person converge upon no other individual; nobody else feels pressure from all five of *his* constituencies; no one else takes pressure in the consciousness that *he* has been elected "by the Nation." Besides, nobody but the President lives day by day with *his* responsibility in an atomic age amidst cold war. And he alone can claim unquestionable right to everybody's information on the mysteries of that age and that war. His place and frame of reference are unique. By the same token, though, his power is mercurial. Since no one shares his place, nobody is committed to uphold what he may do there. The consequences are described by every illustration in this book.

The things a President must think about if he would build his influence are not unlike those bearing on the viability of public policy. The correspondence may be inexact, but it is close. The man who thinks about the one can hardly help contributing to the other. A President who senses what his influence is made of and who means to guard his future will approach his present actions with an eye to the reactions of constituents in Washington and out. The very breadth and sweep of his constituencies and of their calls upon him, along with the uncertainty of their response, will make him keen to see and weigh what Arthur Schlesinger has called "the balance of administrative power." This is a balance of political, managerial, psychological, and personal feasibilities. And because the President's own frame of reference is at once so all-encompassing and so political, what he sees as a balance for himself is likely to be close to what is viable in terms of public policy. Viability requires three ingredients. First is a purpose that moves with the grain of history, a direction consonant with coming needs. Second is an operation that proves manageable to the men who must administer it, acceptable to those who must support it, tolerable to those who must put up with it, in Washington and out. Timing can be crucial for support and acquiescence; proper timing is the third ingredient. The President who sees his power stakes sees something very much like the ingredients that make for viability in policy.

Presidential expertise thus serves effective policy. Deciding what is viable has grown more critical and more complex with almost every turn of world events (and of home politics) since the Second World War. Substantive considerations have become so specialized that experts in one sphere lose touch with expertise in any other. Substantive appraisals have become so tricky that the specialists in every sphere dispute among themselves. In consequence the viability of policy may be the only ground on which a substantive decision can be reached. When that ground is itself inordinately complicated by the tendency of policies to interlock, and overlap, and to leap national boundaries, it becomes a sphere of expertise as specialized as others. In the sphere of viability our system can supply no better expert than a President intent on husbanding his influence—provided that he understands what influence is made of.

The more determinedly a President seeks power, the more he will be likely to bring vigor to his clerkship. As he does so he contributes to the energy of government. In Congress and the agencies and in the national parties, energy is generated by support or opposition. But first there must be something to support or to oppose. Most Washingtonians look to the White House for it. There often is no other place to look. The need of others for a President's initiatives creates dependence on him. Their dependence becomes his advantage. Yet he can only capture the advantage as he meets the need. An energetic clerk will energize all government; the man intent on influence will be that sort of clerk. (So may a man intent on history, provided that he has the heroes of a Harry Truman. But one cannot expect that many men will know their history as well as he, and those who know it may choose other heroes.)

The contributions that a President can make to government are indispensable. Assuming that he knows what power is and wants it, those contributions cannot help but be forthcoming in some measure as by-products of his search for personal influence. In a relative but real sense one can say of a President what Eisenhower's first Secretary of Defense once said of General Motors: what is good for the country is good for the President, and *vice versa*. There is no guarantee, of course, that every President will keep an eye on what is "good" for him; his sense of power and of purpose and the source of his self-confidence may turn his head away. If so, his "contributions" could be lethargy not energy, or policy that moves against, not with, the grain of history. The way he sees his influence and seeks it will affect the rest of us, no matter what becomes of him.

3

The Presidency—Focus of Leadership

CLINTON ROSSITER

In this century the growth and complexity of the domestic economy and the recurring crises abroad have forced burdens and responsibilities upon the President far beyond anything contemplated by the Founding Fathers. Professor Rossiter discusses the varied roles of the modern Chief Execu-

Clinton Rossiter, "The Presidency—Focus of Leadership," New York Times Magazine, November 11, 1956. © 1956 by The New York Times Company. Reprinted by permission.

*tive and his strategic position in giving direction not only to his own
country but to the rest of the world. Yet despite his tremendous power
and prestige, he is subject to the considerable restraints imposed by a
constitutional system and the nation's democratic traditions.*

NO AMERICAN CAN contemplate the Presidency [today] without a feeling
of solemnity and humility—solemnity in the face of a historically unique
concentration of power and prestige, humility in the thought that he
has had a part in the choice of a man to wield the power and enjoy the
prestige.

Perhaps the most rewarding way to grasp the significance of this
great office is to consider it as a focus of democratic leadership. Freemen,
too, have need of leaders. Indeed, it may well be argued that one of
the decisive forces in the shaping of American democracy has been the
extraordinary capacity of the Presidency for strong, able, popular leadership. If this has been true of our past, it will certainly be true of our
future, and we should therefore do our best to grasp the quality of this
leadership. Let us do this by answering the essential question: For what
men and groups does the President provide leadership?

First, the President is *leader of the Executive Branch.* To the extent
that our Federal civil servants have need of common guidance, he alone
is in a position to provide it. We cannot savor the fullness of the President's duties unless we recall that he is held primarily accountable for
the ethics, loyalty, efficiency, frugality and responsiveness to the public's
wishes of the two and one-third million Americans in the national administration.

Both the Constitution and Congress have recognized his power to
guide the day-to-day activities of the Executive Branch, strained and
restrained though his leadership may often be in practice. From the
Constitution, explicitly or implicitly, he receives the twin powers of appointment and removal, as well as the primary duty, which no law or
plan or circumstances can ever take away from him, to "take care that
the laws be faithfully executed."

From Congress, through such legislative mandates as the Budget
and Accounting Act of 1921 and the succession of Reorganization Acts,
the President has received further acknowledgment of his administrative
leadership. Although independent agencies such as the Interstate Commerce Commission and the National Labor Relations Board operate by
design outside his immediate area of responsibility, most of the Government's administrative tasks are still carried on within the fuzzy-edged
pyramid that has the President at its lonely peak; the laws that are

executed daily in his name and under his general supervision are numbered in the hundreds.

Many observers, to be sure, have argued strenuously that we should not ask too much of the President as administrative leader, lest we burden him with impossible detail, or give too much to him, lest we inject political considerations too forcefully into the steady business of the civil service. Still, he cannot ignore the blunt mandate of the Constitution, and we should not forget the wisdom that lies behind it. The President has no more important tasks than to set a high personal example of integrity and industry for all who serve the nation, and to transmit a clear lead downward through his chief lieutenants to all who help shape the policies by which we live.

Next, the President is *leader of the forces of peace and war*. Although authority in the field of foreign relations is shared constitutionally among three organs—President, Congress, and, for two special purposes, the Senate—his position is paramount, if not indeed dominant. Constitution, laws, customs, the practice of other nations and the logic of history have combined to place the President in a dominant position. Secrecy, dispatch, unity, continuity and access to information—the ingredients of successful diplomacy—are properties of his office, and Congress, needless to add, possesses none of them. Leadership in foreign affairs flows today from the President—or it does not flow at all.

The Constitution designates him specifically as "Commander in Chief of the Army and Navy of the United States." In peace and war he is the supreme commander of the armed forces, the living guarantee of the American belief in "the supremacy of the civil over military authority."

In time of peace he raises, trains, supervises and deploys the forces that Congress is willing to maintain. With the aid of the Secretary of Defense, the Joint Chiefs of Staff and the National Security Council—all of whom are his personal choices—he looks constantly to the state of the nation's defenses. He is never for one day allowed to forget that he will be held accountable by the people, Congress and history for the nation's readiness to meet an enemy assault.

In time of war his power to command the forces swells out of all proportion to his other powers. All major decisions of strategy, and many of tactics as well, are his alone to make or to approve. Lincoln and Franklin Roosevelt, each in his own way and time, showed how far the power of military command can be driven by a President anxious to have his generals and admirals get on with the war.

But this, the power of command, is only a fraction of the vast responsibility the modern President draws from the Commander-in-Chief clause. We need only think back to three of Franklin D. Roosevelt's actions in World War II—the creation and staffing of a whole array of emergency boards and offices, the seizure and operation of more than sixty strike-bound or strike-threatened plants and industries, and the forced evacuation of 70,000 American citizens of Japanese descent from the West Coast—to understand how deeply the President's authority can cut into the lives and liberties of the American people in time of war. We may well tremble in contemplation of the kind of leadership he would be forced to exert in a total war with the absolute weapon.

The President's duties are not all purely executive in nature. He is also intimately associated, by Constitution and custom, with the legislative process, and we may therefore consider him as *leader of Congress*. Congress has its full share of strong men, but the complexity of the problems it is asked to solve by a people who still assume that all problems are solvable has made external leadership a requisite of effective operation.

The President alone is in a political, constitutional and practical position to provide such leadership, and he is therefore expected, within the limits of propriety, to guide Congress in much of its lawmaking activity. Indeed, since Congress is no longer minded or organized to guide itself, the refusal or inability of the President to serve as a kind of prime minister results in weak and disorganized government. His tasks as leader of Congress are difficult and delicate, yet he must bend to them steadily or be judged a failure. The President who will not give his best thoughts to leading Congress, more so the President who is temperamentally or politically unfitted to "get along with Congress," is now rightly considered a national liability.

The lives of Jackson, Lincoln, Wilson and the two Roosevelts should be enough to remind us that the President draws much of his real power from his position as *leader of his party*. By playing the grand politician with unashamed zest, the first of these men gave his epic administration a unique sense of cohesion, the second rallied doubting Republican leaders and their followings to the cause of the Union, and the other three achieved genuine triumphs as catalysts of Congressional action. That gifted amateur, Dwight D. Eisenhower, has also played the role for every drop of drama and power in it. He has demonstrated repeatedly what close observers of the Presidency know well: that its incumbent must devote an hour or two of every working day to the profession of Chief Democrat or Chief Republican.

It troubles many good people, not entirely without reason, to watch the President dabbling in politics, distributing loaves and fishes, smiling on party hacks, and endorsing candidates he knows to be unfit for anything but immediate delivery to the county jail. Yet if he is to persuade Congress, if he is to achieve a loyal and cohesive administration, if he is to be elected in the first place (and re-elected in the second), he must put his hand firmly to the plow of politics. The President is inevitably the nation's No. 1 political boss.

Yet he is, at the same time if not in the same breath, *leader of public opinion*. While he acts as political chieftain of some, he serves as moral spokesman for all. It took the line of Presidents some time to sense the nation's need of a clear voice, but since the day when Andrew Jackson thundered against the Nullifiers of South Carolina, no effective President has doubted his prerogative to speak the people's mind on the great issues of his time, to serve, in Wilson's words, as "the spokesman for the real sentiment and purpose of the country."

Sometimes, of course, it is no easy thing, even for the most sensitive and large-minded of Presidents, to know the real sentiment of the people or to be bold enough to state it in defiance of loudly voiced contrary opinion. Yet the President who senses the popular mood and spots new tides even before they start to run, who practices shrewd economy in his appearances as spokesman for the nation, who is conscious of his unique power to compel discussion on his own terms and who talks the language of Christian morality and the American tradition, can shout down any other voice or chorus of voices in the land. The President is the American people's one authentic trumpet, and he has no higher duty than to give a clear and certain sound.

The President is easily the most influential leader of opinion in this country principally because he is, among all his other jobs, our Chief of State. He is, that is to say, the ceremonial head of the Government of the United States, the *leader of the rituals of American democracy*. The long catalogue of public duties that the Queen discharges in England and the Governor General in Canada is the President's responsibility in this country, and the catalogue is even longer because he is not a king, or even the agent of one, and is therefore expected to go through some rather undignified paces by a people who think of him as a combination of scoutmaster, Delphic oracle, hero of the silver screen and father of the multitudes.

The role of Chief of State may often seem trivial, yet it cannot be neglected by a President who proposes to stay in favor and, more to the point, in touch with the people, the ultimate support of all his claims to leadership. And whether or not he enjoys this role, no President can fail to realize that his many powers are invigorated, indeed are given a new dimension of authority, because he is the symbol of our sovereignty, continuity and grandeur as a people.

When he asks a Senator to lunch in order to enlist his support for a pet project, when he thumps his desk and reminds the antagonists in a labor dispute of the larger interests of the American people, when he orders a general to cease caviling or else be removed from his command, the Senator and the disputants and the general are well aware—especially if the scene is laid in the White House—that they are dealing with no ordinary head of government. The framers of the Constitution took a momentous step when they fused the dignity of a king and the power of a Prime Minister in one elective office—when they made the President a national leader in the mystical as well as the practical sense.

Finally, the President has been endowed—whether we or our friends abroad like it or not—with a global role as a *leader of the free nations.* His leadership in this area is not that of a dominant executive. The power he exercises is in a way comparable to that which he holds as a leader of Congress. Senators and Congressmen can, if they choose, ignore the President's leadership with relative impunity. So, too, can our friends abroad; the action of Britain and France in the Middle East is a case in point. But so long as the United States remains the richest and most powerful member of any coalition it may enter, then its President's words and deeds will have a direct bearing on the freedom and stability of a great many other countries.

Having engaged in this piecemeal analysis of the categories of Presidential leadership, we must now fit the pieces back together into a seamless unity. For that, after all, is what the Presidency is, and I hope this exercise in political taxonomy has not obscured the paramount fact that this focus of democratic leadership is a single office filled by a single man.

The President is not one kind of leader one part of the day, another kind in another part—leader of the bureaucracy in the morning, of the armed forces at lunch, of Congress in the afternoon, of the people in the evening. He exerts every kind of leadership every moment of the day, and every kind feeds upon and into all the others. He is a more exalted leader of ritual because he can guide opinion, a more forceful leader in diplomacy because he commands the armed forces personally, a more effective leader of Congress because he sits at the top of his party. The conflicting demands of these categories of leadership give him trouble at times, but in the end all unite to make him a leader without any equal in the history of democracy.

I think it important to note the qualification: "the history of democracy." For what I have been talking about here is not the Fuehrerprinzip of Hitler or the "cult of personality," but the leadership of free men. The Presidency, like every other instrument of power we have created for our use, operates within a grand and durable pattern of private liberty and public morality, which means that the President can lead successfully only when he honors the pattern—by working toward ends to which a "persistent and undoubted" majority of the people has given support, and by selecting means that are fair, dignified and familiar.

The President, that is to say, can lead us only in the direction we are accustomed to travel. He cannot lead the gentlemen of Congress to abdicate their functions; he cannot order our civil servants to be corrupt and slothful; he cannot even command our generals to bring off a coup d'état. And surely he cannot lead public opinion in a direction for which public opinion is not prepared—a truth to which our strongest Presidents would make the most convincing witnesses. The leadership of free men must honor their freedom. The power of the Presidency can move as a mighty host only with the grain of liberty and morality.

The President, then, must provide a steady focus of leadership—of administrators, Ambassadors, generals, Congressmen, party chieftains, people and men of good will everywhere. In a constitutional system compounded of diversity and antagonism, the Presidency looms up as the countervailing force of unity and harmony. In a society ridden by centrifugal forces, it is the only point of reference we all have in common. The relentless progress of this continental republic has made the Presidency our one truly national political institution.

There are those, to be sure, who would reserve this role to Congress, but, as the least aggressive of our Presidents, Calvin Coolidge, once testified, "It is because in their hours of timidity the Congress becomes subservient to the importunities of organized minorities that the President comes more and more to stand as the champion of the rights of the whole country." The more Congress becomes, in Burke's phrase, "a confused and scuffling bustle of local agency" the more the Presidency must become a clear beacon of national purpose.

It has been such a beacon at most great moments in our history. In this great moment, too, we may be confident it will burn brightly.

4

The President as Political Leader

THEODORE SORENSEN

Chief aide and confidential advisor to President Kennedy, Theodore Sorensen discusses from his White House vantage point the vital strands in the fabric of presidential leadership: constant attention to his role as party leader, to public opinion, to pressure groups, to Congress, and to the mass communications media. Most important of all is his responsibility for making ultimate decisions.

WE CAN TURN now to the major forces or sources of influence which shape the presidential decision itself, grouped under three frames of reference: presidential politics, presidential advisers, and the presidential perspective. (All of these classifications are arbitrary and imprecise, and another observer with equal logic and accuracy might well have listed twenty-three or indeed forty-three subdivisions.)

Some purists—if not realists—may blush at the fact that politics heads the list. But we are discussing our prime political office and the nation's prime politician, a man who has been chosen by his party as well as the people. Some Presidents may assert that they are "above politics," yet politics, in its truest and broadest sense, still colors their every decision (including the decision to appear nonpolitical). Some issues have been traditionally deemed to be outside of politics, but considerations of public and congressional support still affect their disposition.

There is nothing dishonorable about the influence of politics on White House decisions. In a nation governed by the consent of the governed, it is both honorable and indispensable. While limitations of responsibility and accuracy should always be present, to say that we should remove such issues as Berlin or Red China from politics is to say they should be removed from public accountability and scrutiny. To charge that a President is politically motivated when he advocates a tax

Theodore C. Sorensen, Decision Making in the White House *(New York: Columbia University Press, 1963), pp. 43-56. Copyright, 1963 by Columbia University Press. Reprinted by permission.*

cut or a strong civil rights measure is simply to charge that he is doing what every elected official is elected to do.

Politics pervades the White House without seeming to prevail. It is not a role for which the President sets apart certain hours. It is rarely the sole subject of a formal presidential meeting. It is instead an ever-present influence—counterbalancing the unrealistic, checking the unreasonable, sometimes preventing the desirable, but always testing what is acceptable.

PUBLIC OPINION

But democratic government is not a popularity contest; and no President is obliged to abide by the dictates of public opinion. Our political idealism may be filled with assumptions of human virtue and wisdom, but our political history is filled with examples of human weakness and error.

Public opinion is often erratic, inconsistent, arbitrary, and unreasonable—with a "compulsion to make mistakes," as Walter Lippmann put it. It rarely considers the needs of the next generation or the history of the last. It is frequently hampered by myths and misinformation, by stereotypes and shibboleths, and by an innate resistance to innovation. It is usually slow to form, promiscuous and perfidious in its affection, and always difficult to distinguish. For it rarely speaks in one loud, clear, united voice.

A President, therefore, must remember that public opinion and the public interest do not always agree. The value to this nation of a foreign aid program, for example, is not determined by its popularity. Last year's trade expansion bill could not have awaited a spontaneous public demand. Voter enthusiasm for our space effort is high after each flight of a Soviet or American astronaut, but in between flights new doubts and complaints will emerge. And almost any pollster in any state will find that most voters want higher federal expenditures in their areas of interest, lower expenditures elsewhere, and a balanced budget always.

No President could simply respond to these pressures. He has a responsibility to lead public opinion as well as respect it—to shape it, to inform it, to woo it, and win it. It can be his sword as well as his compass. An aroused public opinion was more effective in 1962, for example, in helping create a climate favorable to the rescission of steel prices, than any statutory tool. President Kennedy's televised explanations of his decisions on Berlin, nuclear testing, and the Cuban quarantine achieved on each occasion a new national consensus that discouraged any adversary's hopes for disunity.

But arousing public opinion is a delicate task. President Kennedy's plea for fall-out shelters in his 1961 discussion of Berlin ended the prevailing national apathy on civil defense, but it also unleashed an emotional response which grew to near-hysterical proportions (before it receded once again to near-apathy). His warnings on the presence of Soviet missiles in Cuba had to be sufficiently somber to enlist support around the world without creating panic here at home.

In 1961 he resisted the recommendation that he declare a full-scale national emergency over the threat to Berlin, recognizing that this resort to ultimate powers and public response had to be selectively used. For similar reasons, he has generally resisted urgings of disappointed partisans who would have him stir up the public against a Congress which is controlled (at least nominally) by his own party and which has consistently enacted four-fifths of his program.

In short, presidential appeals for public support must be at the right time and with the right frequency, if they are to be effective. On other occasions he may need to alienate a portion of his public support, for serving as President of all the people does not mean offending none of them. But this also cannot be done too often if he is to maintain his position, and it should not be done for meaningless or hopeless causes. President Kennedy may have struck the right balance, for he is criticized, on the one hand, for expanding the powers of his office, sending too much to the Congress, and taking on too many controversies, and, at the same time, for "hoarding" his popularity and recognizing the limitations of a largely lethargic electorate.

One important distinction should be kept in mind. In domestic affairs, a presidential decision is usually the beginning of public debate. In foreign affairs, the issues are frequently so complex, the facts so obscure, and the period for decision so short, that the American people have from the beginning—and even more so in this century—delegated to the President more discretion in this vital area; and they are usually willing to support any reasonable decision he makes.

But public opinion cannot be taken for granted. Some Presidents have tried to change it, others have rushed to catch up with it, but none has repeatedly defied it. "With public sentiment on its side," Lincoln said with some exaggeration, "everything succeeds; with public sentiment against it, nothing succeeds." Franklin D. Roosevelt wrote: "I cannot go any faster than the people will let me." And President Kennedy is acutely aware of Jefferson's dictum: "Great innovations should not be forced on slender majorities."

President Kennedy, for example, has pressed a divided Congress and a contented public to abandon century-old economic precepts and accept a sizable tax cut with a sizable deficit at a time of general prosperity, but, unwilling to be so far out in front of Congress and the country that his program would have no chance, he stretched out the proposed tax cut to avoid a peacetime deficit larger than that of his predecessor.

No President respects public opinion simply out of fear of impeachment or even solely out of a desire for reelection—for the same principle is followed in both his terms. Instead both his conscience and his common sense, both his principles and his political judgment, compel him to seek, to the extent possible, the approval of the voters who elected him and who can defeat his party, the consent of the governed who are affected by his decision and on whose consent its success may depend.

Every President must, therefore, be a keen judge of public opinion. He must be able to distinguish its petty whims, to estimate its endurance, to respond to its impatience, and to respect its potential power. He must know how best and how often he can appeal to the public—and when it is better left undisturbed.

No President reaches that summit of public favor without believing he possesses (and he usually does) an extraordinary instinct for public opinion. He does not rely on the views expressed in his mail, or in public petitions, or by pickets in front of the White House, for they all too often reflect only a tiny organized group. He does not rely on opinion polls, which, outside of testing comparative candidate strengths, are still an inexact measure of the voters' views. He does not rely on the crowds that greet him on his travels, knowing they are usually a disproportionately partisan sample. Nor does he generalize from conversations with visitors, reports from his advisers, or his reading and viewing of mass media. His political intuition is in part an amalgamation of all of these —but he is likely to regard his own invisible antennae as somehow more sensitive than any. (President McKinley, according to Speaker Cannon, retained his popularity by "keeping his ear so close to the ground he got it full of grasshoppers.")

I no longer believe those who say that a poor politician could be a good President, "if he could only be appointed to the job." Without the qualities required of a successful candidate—without the ability to rally support, to understand the public, to express its aspirations—without the organizational talent, the personal charm, and the physical stamina required to survive the primaries, the convention, and the election—no man would make a great President, however wise in other ways he might be.

PRESSURE GROUPS, CONGRESS, AND THE PRESS

Each President must also judge when to oppose or accommodate a single segment of public opinion—a region or state, an occupation or age group, an industry or profession, a pressure group or lobby. Some will have views the President respects, such as nuclear scientists on nuclear tests. Some will have influence he seeks to enlist, such as the organization of older citizens on behalf of his health bill. Some will have sufficient power to cause him concern, at least in their own sphere of influence. (The least respected and least effective lobbies in Washington, I might add, are those which rush forward to testify on every measure of every kind, whether directly related or not to the interests of their members. It is doubtful, for example, that President Roosevelt was either heartened or dismayed by the 1934 resolution of a bankers' organization stating that its members would stand solidly behind the President on all emergency measures that did not infringe on their interests.)

There will always be a small but noisy group of critics intolerant of the gap between hope and possibility, complaining of a lack of leadership when long-awaited measures are not immediately enacted, while an equally small and vocal group will wail that each step forward the President takes is a gross usurpation of power.

The amount of pressure generated by those concerned over import competition must be balanced against the less active but larger number of persons benefiting from both exports and imports. The political or congressional attacks induced by a contractor whose weapons system has been discontinued must be weighed against the long-range costs of continuing an outmoded system.

The task is not always one of choosing between two interests. No President, even if he so wished, could suspend the laws in response to complaints—with respect to desegregation or anti-trust, for example. But he may find it desirable to accept amendments to a tax measure, or to reach informal understandings on concessions regarding a trade bill, in order to secure the passage of those bills with the support of a diverse coalition; or he may warn his appointees against exhibiting an attitude toward business or labor that is so hostile it might dampen the economic climate.

A President's own ties with some economic or other interest group may give him additional bargaining power with that group or reduced influence with another. A President with close ties to business, for example, will meet less resistance to his anti-inflation or anti-trust efforts. On the other hand, while it should not be impossible to find an equitable constitutional formula to settle the church-school aid problem, it is difficult for that formula to be suggested by the nation's first Catholic President.

Pressure groups usually have less direct effect on the President than on his relations with the Congress—a large and separate topic but a major arena of presidential politics. While this discussion is concerned primarily with White House decisions, members of the Congress will inevitably attempt to affect those decisions in much the same way as the White House attempts to affect the decisions of the Congress: i.e., legislators will privately or publicly lobby, pressure, encourage, or discourage the President and his advisers, with respect to his legislative program or budget, both before and after their passage through the Congress.

As is true of public opinion and segments thereof, the views of one or more members of Congress must sometimes be resisted, sometimes reshaped, sometimes ignored, and sometimes accepted, depending not only on the validity of those views but on the power of those who express them and on the extent to which they are shared throughout the Congress. Presidents have differed in the degree of their deference to (or domination of) congressional opinion, according to their own legislative experience, their control of their party, and their party's control of the Congress, but all Presidents since Washington have noted the change in climate that occurs when Congress adjourns.

Finally, presidential politics includes attention to the American press and other media. Their selection and description of particular events—far more than their editorials—help to create or promote national issues, to shape the minds of the Congress and public, and to influence the President's agenda and timing. Ever since George Washington expressed the wish in 1777 "that our Printers were more discreet in many of their publications," our Presidents and the press have engaged in what the jargon of the Cold War would call a "contest for men's minds."

The winning side in this contest is debatable. The advent of television has given the President great resources for directly reaching the public, but even presidential corrections rarely catch up with those misstatements which now and then appear in the press. For example, the great newspaper chain which headlined a totally false scare story about Soviet planes overflying the southeastern United States has never acknowledged its error.

I have often been asked why President Kennedy, unlike his predecessor, should bother to read so many newspapers when so much of their important information and arguments—excluding overseas statements and events that occurred during the night—is at least twenty-four hours old to him. Obviously this would be even more true of weekly and monthly magazines. He reads them, I believe, partly to gain new insights for himself but primarily to know what the public and the Congress are reading, to see how his actions or choices appear to others without his access to the facts. For any President, any politician dependent on public opinion, is concerned with how that opinion is shaped, with how, to use a current phrase, the news is being "managed" in the only place it can be managed, the media editorial offices.

5

The Limits of Presidential Leadership

CHARLES E. JACOB

Despite the widespread conviction that the President is uniquely situated to exercise personal leadership in ways that decisively influence the course of national affairs, the realities of political and institutional life suggest that he is, in fact, seriously circumscribed. Professor Jacob explores and analyzes these limiting factors—interest groups, the weight of tradition, institutional barriers, and the presidential hierarchy itself. Paradoxically, while the occupant of the White House is today more powerful than ever before, he is also less powerful because he is curbed when circumstances require that he be free from restraint.

THE CONVENING OF each new Congress invariably arouses speculation about an abiding institutional relationship in American politics: the measure of presidential leadership successfully exerted over the national

Charles E. Jacob, "The Limits of Presidential Leadership," South Atlantic Quarterly, 62 (Autumn 1963), 461-473. Copyright 1963 by Duke University Press. Reprinted by permission.

legislature. The need for executive leadership is manifest. Five hundred and thirty-five legislators cannot "govern." Nor even—to acknowledge a reality publicized as far back as Woodrow Wilson's classic contribution, *Congressional Government*—can the chairmen of the standing committees of Congress govern in any realistic sense of the word. The peculiar qualities of executive leadership described by the Federalists— unity, continuity, secrecy, dispatch, and superior sources of information —are as relevant today as they were in 1787. Yet, while the legislators themselves recognize their own limitations, the normal congressional attitude is a desire to circumscribe carefully the bounds of presidential leadership. The congressman is grateful for executive requests, policy guidelines, and an administrative budget. Nonetheless, while some executive initiative is accepted as desirable, even necessary, Congress looks upon this initiative as a framework which it feels free to embellish, alter, ignore, or abolish. For a friendly Congress, executive leadership provides focus; for an unfriendly one, it provides a basis for criticism of the other branch. In either case it is indispensable.

On the other hand, the natural attitude of the president is one of commitment to his program in the general form in which he presents it. It took only two years for President Eisenhower to develop this sense of commitment, even though he approached office with a more generous and accommodating attitude than is usual in modern presidents. The confrontation of these two attitudes—presidential commitment and congressional caprice—is rooted basically in neither partisanship nor personalities. It symbolizes, rather, a conflict of institutional roles endemic in a system based upon a separation of powers and functions.

In recent decades the contest of presidential and congressional wills has assumed, like so many other things, the character of a spectator sport in the United States. The pollsters faithfully report on the president's personal popularity and that of his specific programs. The political scientists analyze the make-up of the Congress and the strategy, timing, and tactics of presidential requests. The inside dopesters plumb the depths of congressional and executive personalities, their alliances, antipathies, and negotiations. The press and periodicals keep box scores on the passage or failure of items in the presidential program. In the end, presidential success can be summed up in percentage terms.

All of this activity is understandable and much of it useful to the politically conscious citizen and scholar alike. Yet it results in some misconceptions about American politics. In any sport the chief contenders often assume the center of attention. The contest becomes highly personalized. The outcome is seen largely in terms of the skill of the participants. While personal qualities largely determine the results in tennis and basketball, this is far less true of the presidential-congressional competition. A set of impersonal conditioning factors is at work in the relations between president and Congress, and these factors limit the effectiveness of the most skilful executive. A combination of these factors will reduce a wilful president's techniques of manipulation and image-creation to skills of marginal utility, and Congress will proceed, cheerfully immune to his blandishments.

The traditional tools at the disposal of the president for use in leading Congress may be summarized briefly. The Constitution provides three of these directly: the message power; the veto power; executive control of the sessions of Congress.

Beginning with the provision for an annual report on the State of the Union, the seemingly innocuous message power has been expanded through practice into a rather effective vehicle for the initiation of policy. Modern presidents deliver dozens of messages every year requesting and providing guidelines for major legislation. The veto power has been a potent negative device for, though Congress can override the veto, historically the balance of power in this executive-legislative relationship statistically rests clearly with the president. Moreover, the threat of a veto, delivered for purposes of bargaining, subtly transforms an apparently negative power into a positive one. The constitutional provision by which the president may call Congress into special session is of limited use and potency, normally used for partisan political purposes rather than in the service of genuine legislative need.

Informal, extraconstitutional devices have been more effective in supporting presidential leadership over the years. For the most part, these mechanisms are political in nature rather than legal. A president may seek to bend individual congressmen to his will through the dispensation of patronage. As administrator-in-chief he has still another means of persuading congressmen that his way is the best way. The allocation of federal contracts and the establishment or continuation of federal installations and public works projects in various districts across the nation are matters of keen interest to the congressmen representing these districts. Thus, the president, through his lieutenants, can dispense or withhold this kind of patronage.

If the president cannot buy all the support he needs—and he surely cannot—there are further means of gaining it. The creation of a friendly and accommodating attitude among congressmen can often be accomplished through a selective lending of presidential status. Whether this takes the form of Truman poker parties, Eisenhower golf outings, Kennedy breakfasts, or merely White House conferences witnessed by press and television, the object is the same: to employ the majesty of the presidential office in the service of legislative generalship. Finally, the president may appeal to the nation for support on items of his legislative program. If he can make a good case before his national constituency, he may succeed in bringing popular pressure to bear on Congress.

All of these tactics of presidential leadership are familiar and have long been applied with differing degrees of finesse by modern presidents. And it is incontestable that any president who merits the job *should* spend a large part of his time providing Congress with leadership. My quarrel is not with the fact of good leadership; it is with the assumption that legislative achievement will naturally follow. Leadership is only half of the story. Political leadership is exercised within a particular circumstantial, institutional, and ideological context. It is this fundamental truism that is sometimes not given appropriate emphasis.

Richard Neustadt, sometime of Columbia University, has produced an imaginative, thoughtful, and truly sophisticated book with his *Presidential Power: The Politics of Leadership.* Indeed, it is probably an influential book as such books go. (That its influence radiates beyond the academy is undoubted, since Professor Neustadt was hired as a special assistant to President-elect Kennedy in 1960.) Yet one wonders if Neustadt does not err, if only by tenor and implication, in the stress he places on the potential of personal leadership. The book is a veritable catalogue of maxims for great leaders. We are told that, in order to be an effective leader, the president must guard his professional reputation, tend his various overlapping constituencies (the world, the nation, Washington, D.C., Congress, the press corps and so on), and have a gourmet taste for the spicy dish of politics and political manipulation. We are led to conclude that if he can cultivate all these skills stylishly and educate the people in the bargain, the president is bound to succeed in pulling Congress along in the national interest.

The first two years of the Kennedy administration bear witness to this preoccupation with the possibilities of shrewd leadership. The President established the tone early in his campaign. A Kennedy administration would be a vigorous administration. The country had to get moving again. New Frontiers would be explored. Though the rhetoric reflected a noble ambition, words in turn were reflected by deeds. The executive offices of the capital were leased by bright young men from the universities, the laboratories, and the political precincts. These new officials created a composite image of dedication, energy, and political sagacity. They understood power and were not afraid to use it. The conduct of the White House lobby beguiled advocates of a strong presidency. In liberal circles a new political era was forecast. The excitement and the hopes were understandable, for, undoubtedly, political leadership in the preceding eight years had been sparingly and conservatively exercised. Identifying a host of problems that required prompt attention, the administration fed bills into the congressional hopper at a prodigious rate.

To the credit of this ambitious administration, some important policies were safely piloted through the legislative labyrinth. An Area Redevelopment Act, an omnibus housing bill, a Trade Expansion Act, and a thriving Peace Corps provide exemplary testimony to the far-sighted leadership of the executive. On the other hand, many proposals for legislation judged vital by this administration have foundered in Congress. For those who like statistics, it may be noted that the President succeeded in getting the 87th Congress to pass, in any form, only 46.3 per cent of his legislative requests. Even low percentages underestimate the importance of individual measures which failed of passage. A modest addition to the social welfare structure—medical aid to the aged—remains unpassed. The administration's program of federal educational support and expansion stands untouched. The President's attempt merely to mobilize his administration to meet the problems of the urban, industrial era by establishing a Department of Urban Affairs and Housing was frustrated in Congress. Overproduction in agriculture and the ensuing drain on the treasury by the subsidy system seem destined to be with us indefinitely.

Such a catalogue of unmet needs—by this administration's own standards—may be interpreted as a general criticism of presidential leadership. Of course, tactical errors have been committed. There have been times when the President might have spoken more softly (as when he sought to have the urban affairs proposal discharged from the leonine Senate Government Operations Committee) and times when he could have wielded a bigger stick (as when he failed to fight harder for his aid-to-education programs). Yet I must repeat my earlier contention that the main explanation of failure lies in impersonal, situational factors largely beyond the President's control. A consideration of four recurrent obstacles to presidential leadership sets the agenda for the remaining pages of this essay.

THE PERSISTENCE OF INTERESTS

A fact of life of first importance that effectively limits the discretion of any president in formulating new policies is the vitality of existing group interests. It is not an unfair description of American politics to say that the practical function of politicians at all levels is to serve those interests which exercise the greatest influence over them. This function, in turn, establishes the character of American politics as one of conflict and compromise. At the highest levels of decision making, the president must take account of a variety of competing interests and their strength in Congress. Thus at the very outset he is limited by his own calculations of the possible. Regional, economic, occupational, and ideological interests impinge on calculations of policy. The already complex array of influences is further complicated by the existence of factions within larger group interests. Farmers, for example, pose not one interest but several. Large farmers compete with small; wheat farmers with dairy farmers; the South with the West, and so on. Every administration is expected to have a "farm policy," even though any policy that is not meaningless tends to exalt the interest of one over another of the specialized groups of farmers. A preponderance of these groups is never completely satisfied with the policies they demand of government. Hence, neither the Brannan plan of one administration, nor the soil bank of another, nor the feed grains program of a third really disposes of the conflicting imperatives of the farm interest.

One could extend this analysis of the persistence of interests indefinitely. The tradition of overrepresentation of rural interests greets each new executive as he proposes a policy that smacks of solicitude toward urban problems. The defeat of Mr. Kennedy's proposal for a Department of Urban Affairs and Housing resulted primarily from the fear of many congressmen of the new status to be given the interests of their urban fellow citizens. Since the interests of organized laborers, Negroes, and other minority groups were simultaneously involved, the difficulties inherent in the proposal were magnified. The interests of the medical profession and its allies—highly organized, amply financed, and superbly articulated—have succeeded in preventing or emasculating medical aid and federal health insurance programs for many years. A powerful combination of regional and economic interests has consistently prevented higher taxation of the oil industry through a readjustment of the 27.5 per cent oil depletion allowance.

In sum, there is really no important legislative program the president can propose with disregard to the influence of persistent, established group interests. All major legislative proposals must be a product of balance and compromise if they are to enjoy even half a chance of survival in the legislative struggle. And more often than not, the happiest result for the president will be a slightly advantageous armistice negotiation rather than complete victory.

THE LEGACY OF PAST POLICIES

In large measure every president is held in thrall by the dead hand of past policies. Rare is the revolutionary occasion when sharp departures from a prescriptive legal framework are possible. Often ambitions of presidential leadership in new directions are frustrated by a surprisingly large corpus of existing statutory limitations. The rule of precedent is not confined to the judiciary alone. This kind of inertia has been demonstrated particularly forcefully in budgetary matters. One of President Eisenhower's priorities was to cut spending and reduce the national debt, a quest that resulted in bigger budgets in five years out of eight, with deficits in five years as well. Incremental defense commitments were met. Where the "creeping socialism" of the welfare state might have been arrested in 1954, the social security program was expanded. Rivers and harbors projects and like contents of the traditional pork barrel were annually replenished in those years of fiscal conservatism.

The persistence of interests noted earlier has long been safely reinforced through congressional codification. It might be difficult for President Kennedy to expand certain of these existing programs or augment them with others, but he would face even stronger opposition should he attempt to deny the farm bloc its $5.7 billion or the veterans their $5.5 billion in the new budget. In another context, the President last year briefly threatened to veto the impacted-areas dole of educational aid for communities serving federal installations. He was piqued at the refusal of Congress to pass his general aid-to-education program while retaining the impacted-areas legislation politically useful to individual congressmen as a constituency benefit. Finally, accepting one-tenth of a loaf as better than none, he acceded to congressional generosity.

The demands on modern government are so tenacious and the legal mechanisms for their satisfaction so stable that the range of discretion within which the president can call for policy substitutions is very narrow indeed. He must accept an overwhelming portion of the status quo as a given and lead largely by fostering incremental change. In order to do this he must overcome stern congressional resistance to new policies.

INSTITUTIONAL RESISTANCE IN CONGRESS

Despite the hopes of those who would like to find in executive-legislative relations the basis for a governmental partnership, these relations are more aptly comparable to sustained diplomatic negotiations between two sovereign powers operating under different constitutions and motivated by different sets of conventions. Realistically, Congress should be viewed as it views itself—an independent universe. While the presidency is organized for action, with delay and inaction being the deviant pattern, Congress is organized essentially for delay, with dispatch being the deviant pattern.

The congressional universe is peopled by discrete groups of individuals playing a variety of identifiable roles. There are the leaders who have attained power and exercise it freely, as well as the backbenchers who have little power and can only hope for more after a suitably long apprenticeship in the system. Some are strict party men, always scoring high on the roll-call register of party cohesiveness. Others could scarcely care less about dogmas of party loyalty. The chief preoccupation of the latter is with errand-boy services to their constituents and the maintenance of personal organizations in the provinces. In any case, congressional morality is viewed by the members through lenses focused on the institution itself and the norms it establishes and upholds.

The procedural norms are those familiar conventions of the Congress such as the committee system, the seniority system, the special function of the Rules Committee in the House, and the tradition of unlimited debate in the Senate. The necessary division of labor in a large legislative body makes a system of functionally specialized standing committee a perfectly rational device. In practice, however, the committee becomes a nearly sovereign master in its area of jurisdiction instead of a service group subordinate to the whole body. For the most part, the chairman of the committee exercises its sovereignty. Under the seniority system the eldest surviving members—those normally unbothered by electoral competition and a resulting rejuvenation in political outlook—are the chairmen of the standing committees.

The Rules Committee of the House usually adopts a parsimonious demeanor in its scrutiny of legislative production, and, because of its powerful role in clearing legislation for floor action, is able to exercise an obstructionist function. Unlimited debate in the Senate produces the same delaying actions that committee stratagems do in the House. Thus, the folkways of the chambers exercise a conservative influence on the legislative process. One might ask whether the legislators are not masters of their own houses. Given an expression of strong sentiment in opposition to the cumbersome institutional machinery, could Congress not strip itself down for action? The answer is that, while theoretically this is possible (a modest and not highly successful attempt was made in 1946 with the passage of the Legislative Reorganization Act), it is unlikely for at least two reasons.

First, the inertia of tradition and the imperatives of prescription are deeply felt, especially among the elders. The congressional Establishment is nothing if not a faithful guardian of the integrity of its conventions. Second, and by all accounts more important, *within* the congressional universe all the delaying tactics are of potential use to the legislator as careerist. It is not quite accurate to write off congressional conventions as nothing more than devices susceptible to manipulation by the Establishment. While it is obvious, for example, that the elders have more to gain in the perpetuation of the committee seniority system, access to the Rules Committee, and the weakness of the party signal, it is also true that the most junior M. C. can find aid and comfort in these institutions from time to time. The congressman, pressured by his constituents, may boldly or dutifully introduce an undesirable or innocuous piece of legislation in the secure knowledge that it will never leave the committee or be granted a rule by Judge Howard Smith of the Rules Committee. Lack of party discipline permits the member to vote his conscience—or, more often, his constituents' apparent wishes—in violation of partisan demands. The privilege of unlimited debate and the filibuster in the Senate have been invoked by such unflinching opponents of the principle as Senators Douglas and Morse.

The irony in all this is that although the institutions of Congress, because of their rigidity, fortify resistance to outside leadership on national policy matters, they also provide for more flexibility within Congress by granting the congressman qua congressman a variety of options in pursuing his own natural interest: getting ahead and getting re-elected.

INTERNAL ADMINISTRATIVE DYSFUNCTION

If presidential leadership meets with resistance in Congress because of the essentially different goal orientation and mode of operation of that body, one might assume that the executive can depend on unity of support within the administrative family to help provide guidance and overcome legislative opposition. This is not always the case, as many a president has learned. To understand why this is so, we must recognize immediately that the "administrative family" is not the social worker's ideal of a tightly knit ménage. It is rather a family of many branches in which one branch is often not on speaking terms with another. Originally pure blood lines of administration, over the past eight or ten generations, have been diluted by strange mating customs, and some still stranger mutants have resulted. Clear, departmental organization, having a fount of authority in the presidency and applications of this authority in hierarchic descent, has long since been supplemented by other, less simple forms of organization. Administrative structure in the United States has been characterized by periodic divisions and consolidations among functions and offices. In the late nineteenth century a wholly new form of administration was introduced. With the advent of the Interstate Commerce Commission in 1887, the first of a long series of experiments with independent regulatory agencies began. In an atmosphere of populist sentiment, this administrative form was concocted precisely to remove political (including presidential) controls. While from time to time presidents have been able to exercise influence over these agencies, presidential authority has been effectivly undercut. Moreover, since the president does appoint the commissioners, he has been held abstractly responsible for unpopular acts they performed. Sociological niceties aside, all bureaucracy is somehow seen as executive bureaucracy.

The independence of the agencies confronts the president with more than a few cruel dilemmas. The ability of the president to propose a comprehensive course of action, let us say, in the broad area of fiscal planning is limited by the prerogatives of the "fourth headless branch of government." He should be able to garner the support of the Bureau of the Budget and the Treasury Department, but the Federal Reserve Board (an independent agency) may delay or refuse to adjust the interest rate on borrowing, thus tightening or relaxing the credit supply in discord with "administration" policy. Clearly, presidential leadership can be circumscribed by administrative opposition.

The size and complexity of the administrative structure itself is a source of dysfunction. With the growth of federal bureaucracy, intimate political relations are often conducted at the lower levels in a subsystem composed of bureau chiefs on one side and congressional committee chairmen on the other. Gradually, the community of interests and the working interdependence of these nearly autonomous functionaries are reinforced, and the result is often a closer relationship between bureau and committee than between bureau and president. This is particularly true of certain clientele departments and bureaus such as agriculture, commerce, and labor. Policy relating to these departments is often formulated or strongly influenced at the bureau-committee level. Significantly, it is at this juncture that clientele interest groups seek access most avidly.

Effectiveness of presidential control over administration is further diminished by three other institutional phenomena: (1) Interagency competition and rivalry often disrupt the channels of the presidential-congressional communications system. Most notable, though not unique, is the long history of the rivalry among the various branches of the armed services. The claims of the Air Force, for example, are assured a friendly reception by certain legislators whatever the comprehensive strategic policy of the administration may be. Just last year President Kennedy and Defense Secretary McNamara found themselves involved in a costly battle with Representative Carl Vinson, chairman of the House Armed Services Committee, over the executive decision to abandon the RS-70 aircraft project. (2) Congressional control over agency budgets creates a natural dependence by the agency on the committees holding the purse strings. In order to protect the integrity of his bureau or agency, the administrative official may have to resign himself to the expressed congressional view of things, even though this may not be consonant with executive guidelines. (3) Finally, the very existence of the administrative complex arouses congressional suspicions. The specter of Big Bureaucracy haunts the legislative universe. The prospect that new policies must inescapably be administered by *les fonctionnaires*—the natural enemies of congressmen—is sometimes enough to incline the congressional balance toward opposition to these policies.

It is thus a vexatious paradox that, although the president's executive aides participate in the process of providing leadership, the administrative establishment, in part, also blocks that leadership. For a variety of reasons—some unintentional, others built into the complex of institutional relationships—administrative dysfunction contributes a share to leadership frustration.

I have been concerned to argue in this essay that the leadership of the president is essentially situational. This line of argument has been stated frankly in reaction to an exaggeration of the potential of personal qualities of leadership. In the process of sketching out certain categories of rather formidable and persistent limits on presidential leadership, I have not intended to underplay either the possibility or the need for vigorous, astute leadership. Nonetheless, sanguine expectations about the effectiveness of an atomic-age philosopher-king can lead only to disappointment and perhaps—even more portentous in the long run—disenchantment with pluralistic democracy.

It is instructive to recall that the kind of high-potency leadership demanded by some commentators today has been successfully exercised only to the accompaniment of the catalyst of crisis. Wars and depressions have been the conditioning situations that historically permitted nearly unlimited presidential domination of Congress. To those who contend that there are indeed conditions of crisis in our society and our times, I would reply that crisis must be widely perceived in order to be effective as a spur to political action. We can learn, as we recently have from numerous studies that 20 to 25 per cent of our people exist in conditions below the line of poverty. But since the areas of poverty are widely dispersed, isolated, and—more important—excluded from the mainstream of our continental communications network, the news (when heard at all) is accepted as one of those remote statistics by a *predominantly* prosperous and satisfied people. Poverty is simply not perceived except by those who suffer its debilities. And they do not constitute a majority.

Manifestly, it is the duty of a strong president to dramatize such conditions before Congress and the people and call for appropriate action. Unfortunately, however, there are many such "crises." Whether one identifies poverty as our chief crisis, or civil rights, or Cuba, the fact is that there are many such conditions which cry for executive leadership. Even presidential impact is exhaustible. There is a limit to the number of causes that can be exhorted at one time, and the attention span of both Congress and citizenry is decidedly limited. It would seem that one major campaign at a time is about all that can effectively be conducted.

In a democracy policies change slowly; in a pluralistic democracy they change even more slowly. Major policy innovations are finally brought about by majorities, and the majorities must be persistent and undoubted. The limits on presidential leadership are the limits imposed by a plurality of competing interests and institutions. Only through a sacrifice of pluralistic democracy—as we have come to understand it—can all the limits on presidential leadership—as we have identified them—be removed.

6

More Power to the President, Not Less

LOUIS W. KOENIG

The twentieth century pattern of vigorous presidential leadership has sparked a widespread apprehension that an excess of authority may ultimately threaten American democracy. Most professional observers of the Presidency, however, do not share this feeling. Professor Koenig, for example, argues to the contrary. He believes that the President is unduly limited in the exercise of power by such factors as the seniority system in Congress, the twenty-second amendment, the nature of the congressional constituency, and congressional control over foreign policy.

In his view, the United States will be caught up in three major revolutions in the next several decades—the revolutions in human rights, in automation, and in nuclear weapons. If the nation is to cope adequately with these tremendous challenges, the Constitution must be amended and Congress reformed to enable the President, who alone is suited to the task, to make a satisfactory response in a new age.

WHEN LYNDON BAINES JOHNSON is sworn in as President on Jan. 20, attention will again be focused upon this most important office in the land. Although the office is one of great strength, it also has serious weaknesses. In his major roles as party chief, legislative leader, administrative chief and others, the President's capacity to act is bounded with limitations. It is important that in the exhilaration of the coming inaugural, and in the bright glow of Mr. Johnson's remarkable electoral victory, these limitations are not overlooked.

Their seriousness must also be appreciated against the background of hope and concern with which millions will view the new Presidential term—those who face unemployment, or are short-changed in their rights, or have little access to the banquet tables of the affluent society, or fear for mankind's future in the spread of nuclear competence among the nations—all these and countless others. Upon the American President,

Louis W. Koenig, "More Power to the President (Not Less)," New York Times Magazine (January 3, 1965). © by The New York Times Company. Reprinted by permission.

more than upon any other figure in the world, are centered man's hopes and fears for survival, freedom and the good life.

By no means do all Americans view the power of the executive with equal expectation and trust. A suspicion is firmly woven into American tradition, an apprehension that the President either has already appropriated, or someday will appropriate, too much authority and responsibility. In our society the legislature has been viewed—and rightly so—as a champion of liberty, the province of the state governments is substantial, and the economy is chiefly one of private enterprise.

That the Presidency already possesses excessive power was a major contention in the 1964 electoral campaign. In an address to the American Political Science Association on Sept. 11 in Chicago, Senator Goldwater deplored the expansion of executive power at the expense of the other branches of government. He took to task those who hailed the concept of the "strong" Presidents as having a "totalitarian philosophy that the end justifies the means." "We do not want oppressive powers in the hands of the executive branch," he said at Charlotte, N. C., later in the campaign. "We do want the proper balance between all branches and all levels."

Senator Goldwater, who in a real sense was running against the Presidency rather than for it, was articulating a historic sentiment. The 22d Amendment was added to the Constitution in 1951, to cries that it was imperative to limit the President to two terms in order to prevent him from becoming a dictator. All this notwithstanding the fact that no dictator has appeared in the long experience of the American Presidency. In actuality, as public discussion made clear, the amendment was a posthumous attack upon Franklin D. Roosevelt.

The 22d Amendment is a tragedy whose full dimensions are yet to be known. It is clear enough already that it inhibits Presidential power in the second term and shifts the balance to Congress. Dwight Eisenhower has been the first and only victim, as yet, of the amendment's provisions, and he was made very conscious of its impact. In 1957, the first year of his second term, there was a noticeable weakening of his grip on Republican legislators and a softening of his hitherto strong support from the press and business, though he had been returned to power with a fresh and overwhelming mandate.

There have been other serious attempts to limit Presidential power. The Bricker Amendment, also of the nineteen-fifties and pushed for years by tireless promoters, would in effect have prevented the Chief Executive from making treaties and executive agreements with foreign governments. It would have largely shut off the Presidency from foreign affairs.

Not a few Presidents, in using their powers, have engaged in conscious acts of self-denial. President Eisenhower came into office in 1953 imbued with a sense of duty to restore to Congress power which he believed had gravitated unduly from that body to the President in the era of Franklin Roosevelt. Many a 19th-century President shared the view of James Buchanan, who said, "My duty is to execute the laws . . . and not my individual opinions." When Congress did little in the face of gathering rebellion, Buchanan too did little.

When the realities of Presidential power are examined more closely, they reveal an office far less strong than those who attack it would lead us to suppose. A considerable chasm stretches between the Presidency that its critics speak of—or imagine—and the Presidency of reality.

That the Presidency should be a limited office was part of the original conception. Distrustful of power in human hands, the Founding Fathers wrote the principles of checks and balances and separation of powers into the Constitution. Neither Congress nor the executive was to become dominant, but each shared powers of the other, whether making laws, appointments or treaties, and each therefore could check the other (and the Supreme Court could check both).

The President cannot long maintain important policies, domestic or foreign, without Congressional support in the form of laws or money. But whereas a British Prime Minister, with an absolute majority in the House of Commons operating under an altogether different political arrangement can count on legislative enactment of 100 per cent of his proposals, the President does well (except in time of crisis, when he does far better) to average between 50 and 60 per cent.

He will sustain defeats on key measures, as Lyndon Johnson did in 1964 on health care for the aged under Social Security and aid for the depressed Appalachian region. John Kennedy, at the time of his death, still was deprived of legislation he deemed of highest importance—public school aid, civil rights, Medicare, a Cabinet-level urban affairs department and stand-by authority to lower income taxes. Even with a slender majority of four votes, Harold Wilson launched in the first weeks of his Prime Ministership an ambitious and controversial foreign and domestic program, while simultaneously surviving votes of confidence.

The President has no dependable way, as the British Prime Minister does, to command the legislature's support. A complex of forces prompts Congress to resist or oppose the President much of the time. Because the method of electing the President differs from the method of electing Congressmen, their constituencies and therefore their concerns and viewpoints differ.

The President and Vice President alone are chosen by the nation. Senators and Congressmen are essentially local officers responsible to the voters of a single state or Congressional district. Congress neither chooses the President nor is chosen by him, and is therefore not beholden to him, and cannot be bullied by him.

Only once in four years are the President and members of the House of Representatives elected simultaneously, and even then only one-third of the Senate is elected. At the President's midterm, the House and another one-third of the Senate are chosen, usually with local issues predominating. The outcome more often than not worsens the President's own party support in both Congressional houses. At no point in any four-year term does the President face a Senate wholly elected during his tenure, owing to the Senate's six-year term and staggered elections. Presidents come and go, but the most powerful legislators—the chairmen of the standing committees—stay on, often for a third of a century and more.

The likelihood is that a President who seeks important—and therefore controversial—social and economic legislation will face a hard wall of opposition from legislative leaders of his own party. These are the committee chairmen who have great seniority because they come from "safe" districts, situated chiefly in Southern and in rural and small-town areas.

The House Rules Committee chairman in 1964, Howard W. Smith, a small-town Virginian, has, over three decades, compiled an imposing record of thwarting Presidential legislation. He helped bottle up Franklin Roosevelt's wage and hour bill, fought off most of Truman's Fair Deal program, and throttled education and welfare measures of both the Eisenhower and Kennedy Administrations.

Mr. Smith's fellow Southerners dominated the committee chairmanships in 1964. Of 20 standing committees in the House, 12 were led by Southerners and Southwesterners. The disproportion was even greater in the Senate, where legislators from the same regions ran 12 out of 16 committees. It has been aptly said that although the South lost the Civil War, it has never lost the U. S. Senate.

The 1964 Democratic landslide had no particular impact on the roster of Congressional committee chairmen. All the House chairmen in the 88th Congress who were renominated were re-elected. The same is true in the Senate. The 89th Congress, commencing tomorrow, will find Howard Smith back at his old stand on the House Rules Committee, Harry Byrd of Virginia on the Senate Finance Committee, James Eastland of Mississippi on the Senate Judiciary Committee, and so on.

Although the Founding Fathers did not foresee political parties, their rise has not hampered in any significant way the intended effect of checks and balances. President Eisenhower once perceptively observed, "Now let's remember there are no national parties in the United States. There are . . . state parties."

Our parties function effectively as national organizations only when control of the White House is at stake. Otherwise, a party is a loose confederation of state and local organizations, with sectional cleavages and factional differences commonplace. The President and the legislators, although they wear the same party label, are nominated by different party organizations and are chosen by different electorates, an arrangement that hardly works for unity.

There is no common standard of party loyalty, and no party caucus, as in Great Britain which joins the executive with the legislators of his party in common support of a program. Even in the crisis of an election, which presumably would bring the party and its members into closest unity, differences between the President and his Congressional party colleagues may rush to the surface.

The lengths to which the maladies may go is suggested by an episode midway in Eisenhower's second term, during the Congressional elections of 1958. Richard M. Simpson of Pennsylvania, then chairman of the Republican Congressional Campaign Committee, went so far as to counsel Republican candidates for the House of Representatives to forget about Eisenhower's favor and support and "make known" to voters any "disagreement with the President's policies." Simpson, a conservative Republican, often opposed the President's "modern Republicanism."

Checks and balances and the President's legislative and party weaknesses affect his other functions. Although political science textbooks like to refer to him as "administrative chief," Congress too has powers over administration which it can use with the same independence that it exercises over legislation.

It can vest authority in subordinate officials to act independently of higher leadership, stratify a department's internal organization and require Senate confirmation of bureau chiefs. It can create independent regulatory commissions, such as the Interstate Commerce Commission and the Federal Reserve Board, rather far-removed from the President's control. Congress establishes the missions of departments, authorizes and amends their programs and provides money in such amounts and with such strings attached as it chooses.

Even where his authority is presumably great, in foreign affairs and as Commander in Chief, the President depends on Congressional support. He often encounters resistance; George F. Kennan, surveying his tenure as Ambassador to Yugoslavia, was driven to remonstrate that "without the support of Congress, it was impossible to carry out an effective policy here."

The requirement that two-thirds of the Senate approve treaties makes the President vulnerable to concessions and reservations and puts him to the difficult test of winning support from the opposition party. Significantly, it was at the request of the Senate Republican leader, Everett Dirksen, that President Kennedy sent a letter to the Senate, when the test ban treaty was in its hands, giving a series of "assurances" to win over uncertain votes.

That the Presidency, for all the chains it wears, has served us well is not in question. It has waged and won wars, checked depressions, spread social justice, and spurred the nation's growth. But the great crises in the nation's past have tended to come singly and intermittently, and fortunately have been of limited duration.

Our future promises to be quite another matter. It does not require a crystal ball to see that the United States will be engrossed over the next several decades in a simultaneous confrontation of at least three kinds of revolutions: the human rights revolution, the automation revolution and the weapons revolution. None will be short-term. All are enduring phenomena, capable of spawning innumerable subrevolutions; all are apt to be sources of pervasive change for the world, the nation and the lives of each of us.

The human rights revolution is only beginning. President Johnson's announced dedication to equal opportunity for all Americans, regardless of race, will require deep transformations of long prevailing realities in fields such as employment, health, education, housing and recreation. Merely one clue to the magnitude of this task is the fact that nearly 45 per cent of the nation's Negro citizens live in poverty—that is, they have yearly incomes of under $2,000.

We must be prepared to face the possibility that the automation revolution, whose marvels are already well apparent, may, as it gains momentum, increase unemployment to such a degree that the traditional link between jobs and income will be broken. The electronic computer and the automated, self-regulating machine may largely invalidate the general mechanism that undergirds our rights as consumers. Social attitudes toward work and leisure and the basis of individual compensation will need to undergo fundamental revisions.

No less initiative will be required in foreign affairs to make reason prevail over the horrendous alternative of nuclear war. The severity of the problem is already emerging in clear outline with Secretary of Defense McNamara's prediction of a steadily increasing spread of nuclear weapons capability among the nations in coming decades. The clear likelihood is that the adequacy of alliances and the United Nations, and the utility of national sovereignty in such a world, will be brought into serious question.

In the face of these and other possible revolutions, the task of future American leadership is clear. Peoples must be aroused, Congress moved, the bureaucracy stirred and alliances redirected. Only the President can do it.

To enable the Presidency to stay with the race, and to provide the nation, the world and mankind creative and forceful responses for the towering problems of the nineteen-sixties and beyond, several things might well be done to strengthen the office.

1. The present uneven terms of the President, Senate and House might be replaced by the simultaneous election of all three for an identical term of four years. Past elections suggest that an election so conducted might produce a President and two houses of Congress in better harmony on party and policy outlook than the present fragmented elections permit.

2. The President should be given the item veto for appropriation bills. The item veto would equip him with powerful new bargaining strength which he could employ widely to advance his policies on Capitol Hill. He could conceivably engage in a kind of "log-rolling," exchanging his acceptance of appropriation items for support of his own measures by legislators individually and in blocs. The item veto might give the President a truly commanding influence in legislative affairs.

3. The seniority principle of choosing committee chairmen, which almost assures that a preponderance of those eminences will oppose much of the President's program, urgently needs to be modified. Chairmen might well be chosen by secret ballot of a majority of the entire committee at the beginning of each new Congress. The Speaker might have restored his former power to appoint the chairman and members of the House Rules Committee. A time limit might be placed on the number of weeks or months committees might consider and "bottle up" bills.

4. If the treaty power were revised to require the approval of only a majority of Senators present, rather than two-thirds, the President would be less vulnerable to pressures for concessions and reservations in the treaty's development and approval.

5. The 22d, or two-term, Amendment should be repealed.

6. More frequent national party conventions, a national party council or cabinet, the stimulation of regional rather than local organizations, steps toward greater national party financing, all would capitalize on several trends afoot toward stronger national party organizations.

7. Future Presidents might continue what Kennedy began in subordinating party and Congressional politics to urban politics. Kennedy pitched his policies, such as civil rights, education, housing and the like, to urban, racial, national and economic groups. Thereupon he could confidently cultivate state and local party leaders who determine the selection of and the support given to Congressional candidates. Local leaders, whose business it is to win elections, presumably would choose Congressional condidates responsive to the policy needs of urban groups. Kennedy, had he lived to follow his formula through, doubtless would have lighted bonfires under Congressmen and Senators, finding his fuel in the urban groups and local party chieftains.

These proposals will require constitutional amendments, creative Presidential maneuver and serious Congressional reform and party reorganization, all of which admittedly is a very large order. We can console ourselves that other American generations have mastered great problems with bold measures; and we can take a long stride forward and ease the remainder of our task if we disabuse ourselves of the notion that the President has too much power.

7

Creative Presidency, Shadow Presidency

JAMES MACGREGOR BURNS

Presidential government is now a fact of American life. Professor Burns suggests that in the decades to come it will be necessary for the Chief

James MacGregor Burns, Presidential Government: The Crucible of Leadership *(Boston: Houghton Mifflin Co., 1966), pp. 335-345. Copyright Houghton Mifflin Co., 1966. Reprinted by permission.*

Executive to exercise more creative leadership if the social, economic, and cultural malfunctions of contemporary society are to be ameliorated. The President will have to use all available resources for the necessary innovations in numerous areas of public concern. At the same time, if the national purpose is to be served, there must be a vigorous political opposition willing to engage in a constructive dialogue about the course the country is to take. Professor Burns argues for the necessity of imaginative, even daring leadership in the White House.

PEOPLE WERE FREELY predicting at the time of Lyndon Johnson's inaugural in January, 1965, that the nation was headed for a modern era of good feelings. The President himself had said after his election that the country had reached a new "consensus on national purpose and policy." He was quite right—the nation had indeed reached a consensus over the goals of freedom and equality. But these are not the only problems that occupy men, and history warned that eras of apparent good feelings could conceal heats and ferments that would erupt in turbulence and strife years later.

And an unblinking look at the world and the nation in the mid-sixties disclosed a profusion of interlaced problems, any one cluster of which could occupy a people's energies: at home the problems of rapidly changing group and class and generational relationships, education, urban disorder, mounting crime rates, social anomie and alienation, automation, political apathy, along with the more old-fashioned issues such as transportation, farm subsidies, labor-management relations, tax reform, monopoly and administered prices, medical care; and abroad, nuclear proliferation, the continuing and in many areas deepening poverty of tens of millions, the population explosion, the disruption of old rural cultures and the flood of people into the restless cities, the fragmentization of Africa, the social unrest of Latin America, communist expansion in Asia, along with the week-to-week "little" crises, any one of which could explode into a major one.

It was impossible in the mid-sixties to predict in what forms these problems would emerge with the passage of time. One might speculate, though, that many of the most crucial domestic problems might revolve around certain old but still compelling value-questions. Given the trends in the nation that one could predict with the greatest certainty—huge population increases in the urban and suburban areas, accelerated social mobility, a constantly enlarging and increasingly homogenized middle-class population, a decline in ethnic solidarity and variety—one might guess that once the old problems of equality and freedom had been subdued, sharper questions might emerge over the possibilities of individuality and privacy in a mass culture. If the past century has seen the early tension and later partial reconciliation of values of liberty and equality, we might be at the threshold of an age increasingly preoccupied with the relation of liberty and fraternity, of privacy and community, of the individual and the group. If in past years we have been concerned with mainly quantitative problems—the amount of goods and services produced and how they were distributed—we might be more occupied in the future with the quality of American life in a great, affluent, complacent, and perhaps mediocre society.

The quality of American life—this is not a new phrase nor a new political issue. It is older than Jefferson's dreams and as young as the Great Society. No one has defined the hope and the promise better than President Johnson. "The great society," he proclaimed at the University of Michigan in May 1964, "is a place where every child can find knowledge to enrich his mind and enlarge his talents. It is a place where leisure is a welcome chance to build and reflect, not a feared cause of boredom and restlessness. It is a place where the city of man serves not only the needs of the body and the demands of commerce, but the desire for beauty and the hunger for community.

"It is a place where man can renew contact with nature. It is a place which honors creation for its own sake and for what it adds to the understanding of the race. It is a place where men are more concerned with the quality of their goals than the quantity of their goods. But most of all, the Great Society is not a safe harbor, a resting place, a final objective, a finished work. It is a challenge constantly renewed, beckoning us toward a destiny where the meaning of our lives matches the marvellous products of our labor."

The crux of the problem is whether a system of presidential government so perfectly adapted to, and so largely facilitative of, quantitative liberalism—that is, of the augmentation and fairer distribution of goods—can redefine its purpose and shift its strategy in order to embrace new values with their implications for changes in means and instrumental goals. Such a shift calls for much more than making the White House into a showplace of the arts, or awarding medals to heroes of culture, or bestowing presidential recognition on private cultural enterprises. It means a concerted and sustained and expensive effort to impart values like those of Johnson to the barren lives of millions of Americans, middle class as well as deprived. It means diverting the kind of resources into cultural, recreational, and educational activities that we have in the past poured into economic recovery, or even into national defense. And such an effort might be controversial and even unpopular. Many Americans would oppose it and deride it; by its very nature such an effort would bring foolish blunders and mishaps that could be easily caricatured; and certain ventures—perhaps an effort to improve the quality of commercial radio and television—could precipitate clashes with powerful interests.

Above all, the shift from the pursuit of quantitative to qualitative goals would call for comprehensive, sustained, and broadly unified policies—in short, for planning. Effective planning is impossible except in the context of at least a rough ordering of values, instrumental goals, and means. It will be as important to have clearly thought out, long-range priorities in this respect as it would be in planning increased productivity. Winston Churchill once said that "those who are possessed of a definite body of doctrine and of deeply rooted convictions upon it will be in a much better position to deal with the shifts and surprises of daily affairs than those who are merely taking short views, and indulging their natural impulses as they are evoked by what they read from day to day." * Considering the intractable nature of the many human problems implicit in the quest for a qualitatively great society, Churchill's remarks are as relevant to a cultural strategy as to a foreign or economic one.

Presidential government is a superb planning institution. The President has the attention of the country, the administrative tools, the command of information, and the fiscal resources that are necessary for intelligent planning, and he is gaining the institutional power that will make such planning operational. Better than any other human instrumentality he can order the relations of his ends and means, alter existing institutions and procedures or create new ones, calculate the consequences of different policies, experiment with various methods, control the timing of action, anticipate the reactions of affected interests, and conciliate them or at least mediate among them.** If, as Hubert Humphrey has said, we need not a planned society but a continuously planning society, the Presidency provides strong and versatile tools for that purpose.

Still, we must acknowledge that the Presidency has become an effective planning agency for reasons of chance as well as volition. In this

* Quoted by W. W. Rostow, "The Planning of Foreign Policy," School of Advanced International Studies, The Johns Hopkins University.
** Cf. David Braybrooke and Charles E. Lindblom, *A Strategy of Decision* (New York: Free Press of Glencoe, 1963).

century the Presidency has been the center of the conflict between labor and capital and later between segregationists and civil rights forces; it has steeled its will and its ideology in the struggles against Nazi tyranny and communist expansion. After a century of planless growth the Presidency found its place as a key part of the American system of ends and means. The question is whether presidential government can detach itself enough from set ideas and existing institutions and old ways in order to embrace new goals. With leadership, to quote Selznick further, "the problem is always *to choose key values and to create a social structure that embodies them.* The task of building values into social structure is not necessarily consistent, especially in early stages, with rules of administration based on economic premises. Only after key choices have been made and related policies firmly established can criteria of efficient administration play a significant role. Even then, the smooth-running machine must accept disturbance when critical problems of adaptation and change arise." *

To define new goals, to fashion new institutions to realize those goals, to avoid both utopianism and opportunism, to build popular support without improper manipulation, to allow for flexibility of means and redefinition of ends, and always to elevate purpose over technique —all this is the test of creative leadership. It will be the test of presidential government in the years ahead. To define leadership in this way is to see the importance of a number of proposals that have been made to strengthen the Presidency and hence to enable the President to reshape institutions and processes: four-year terms for Representatives (to bring presidential and congressional constituencies into closer correspondence); the granting of full power to the President to control executive department organization; finding means of attracting the highest talent to the executive department, especially to its major staff positions; efforts to bring into the policy-making process intellectuals with creative and innovative gifts; providing the President with greater discretionary power over fiscal policy, including the item veto and the granting of authority to change tax rates within certain limits; and above all, the further strengthening of the elected leadership of Congress so that it can act more quickly and comprehensively in harmony with the President. But the greatest need of presidential government does not lie in this kind of reform. We can expect many of these changes to take place in any event as the Presidency becomes increasingly institutionalized. In-

* Philip Selznick, *Leadership in Administration* (Evanston: Row, Peterson and Company, 1957), p. 60.

deed, some are already taking place, in substance if not in form. Some of them at best will simply speed up transitions that already are under way—for example, greater presidential control of fiscal policy.

The greatest need of the Presidency in the years ahead will not lie in internal changes, important though these are, or even in its relations with Congress. The greatest need will be an opposition that challenges presidential values, presidential methods, presidential institutions, that is eager to take power and to present its own definition of the national purpose.

Of all the vital elements of American democratic government the national opposition is the most disorganized, fragmented, and ineffective. As a responsible opposition to the President, Congress is an almost total failure. Hostile Senators and Representatives bombard the White House from all directions. Typically they fail to advance alternative proposals and hence they do not provide the voters with an idea as to how the opposition would govern if it got the chance. The congressmen usually prefer to play the game of bargain and even various forms of genteel blackmail with the President rather than to criticize forthrightly and dramatically. No wonder that Presidents in recent years have been far more sensitive to criticism in the press than on Capitol Hill.

There are good reasons for the debility of the opposition. In part it is a simple reflection of the power of presidential government. "The aggrandizement of the President, especially by the electronic media," as Key has said, "has made the dispersed minority leadership one of low public visibility." * The main difficulty is the bifurcation of the opposition into the presidential and congressional parties. Once the presidential candidate—the presidential party's leader—has made his strenuous campaign and lost, he then becomes "titular" leader of the whole party. This is a polite term for shelved or even repudiated. For once the campaign is lost, the congressional party leaders try to assume the opposition role. They hold formal and visible positions from which to conduct the attack, while the titular leader usually has no formal position to fall back on, as in the cases of Stevenson in 1956, Nixon in 1960, and Goldwater in 1964. But the congressional party cannot carry the burden of militant leadership, because of its own internal divisions, its separation between the House and the Senate, and its lack of institutional structure (as compared with the Shadow Cabinet in Great Britain). If the opposition party has lost the Presidency but still controls one or both branches of Congress, as in the case of the Democrats after

* V. O. Key, Jr., *Public Opinion and American Democracy* (New York: Alfred A. Knopf, 1961), p. 457.

1956, it lacks the advantage of being completely in the opposition; it suffers from having a modicum of power and responsibility. If the opposition party lacks control of Congress as well as of the White House, it has a poor forum from which to appeal to the public and virtually no machinery to support a focused and sustained attack on the government.

The impotence of the opposition becomes more serious as presidential government becomes more powerful. No matter how benign a government may be, it will be tempted to manipulate public opinion, to try to dominate the flow of opinion, to cover up mistakes, and to cast doubt on the patriotism or at least the honesty of outside critics. The more that government represents a consensus, or claims to, the more tempted it may be to succumb to some of these tendencies. Above all a consensus government may become flabby and complacent and lose the cutting edge of energy, initiative, and innovation. The very tendencies toward excessive concern with technique that we noted above can cause a government to lose direction and momentum unless the opposition holds it to its promises and threatens to oust it from power.

The problem is especially acute in the United States because of the lack of well organized and programmatic parties. This is less of a problem for the President because, as we have seen, he has built up his own presidential party to provide him with an electoral footing and other political resources. The opposition presidential party, lacking a President and having to make do with a titular leader, is not anchored in an organized mass following and a militant cadre; it must improvise—and that in turn encourages a similar opportunism and absence of direction in the presidential establishment.

The greatest need of the American Presidency is a potent and competitive Shadow Presidency. At the very least the opposition party should establish some kind of collective leadership modeled perhaps after the Democratic Advisory Council of the 1950's, to give the presidential party a strong voice. More than this, it should experiment with an annual or biennial convention or conference both to choose a top leader and to renovate its program. The failure of the opposition to take this primitive step is not due to any innate difficulty but mainly to the divergent constituencies and institutional jealousies of the congressional party which wants to dominate the opposition role even though it fills that role so feebly. Ideally there would be an annual convention, a dependable system for collecting adequate funds, a large national staff with regional and state units under it, an effective propaganda apparatus, and talented, articulate, and highly visible leadership. Whatever the exact form, it is clear that the opposition party today has a rare opportunity to exercise Jeffersonian leadership—that is, to build a new political institution.

Even more important, the opposition party must display creative leadership in defining its own version of the national purpose. It is not for outsiders to lecture the opposition party as to the goals it might propose, but one must note the great opportunity that may lie before it. If presidential government as shaped by liberals for egalitarian purposes cannot shift its own strategy toward qualitative goals, if presidential government under Democratic party leadership may be hobbled by its own successes, then the opposition could seize the initiative. American conservatives have long been interested in the now intensifying problems of individuality and community, identity and alienation, liberty and fraternity, innovation and tradition, equality and hierarchy. As Clinton Rossiter has argued, they have not blinked at the hard questions about man in society. And it was under Abraham Lincoln and Theodore Roosevelt, both Republicans, that the nation first addressed itself most directly to problems of the quality of American life. In executing one of the oldest of political and military strategies—shifting the very grounds of the combat—modern conservatives can come to grips with liberal Democracy and its presidential establishment.

Perhaps all this is unnecessary—perhaps we can give in to the acknowledged rewards and virtues of presidential government, without worrying much about competition, criticism, alternatives, and the tasks of an opposition. But a great people will not be content long to float in such a slack tide.

8

How to Pick a President

SIDNEY WARREN

The criteria that should be considered in choosing a President, Professor Warren suggests, are different from those which apply to executive leadership in business or professional life. A candidate cannot "train" for the office in the usual sense of preparing for a career. The important quali-

Sidney Warren, "How to Pick a President," Saturday Review (July 4, 1964). Reprinted by permission.

ties are his view of the Presidency, his zest and an ability for leadership,
his willingness to use the available devices of power, his capacity to make
decisions, his political skill, his humanitarian approach in solving the
problems affecting society, and a sense of the trend of historical forces.

IS THERE ANY way for the American people to determine whether a potential President will provide effective leadership? What standards should
be applied in selecting a candidate for the highest office in the land?
When a business organization seeks a man for a top job, the applicant's
background, training, and experience are major factors in evaluating his
competence. But how useful are these criteria for judging the future head
of state?

In his incisive commentary on American political institutions, *The
American Commonwealth,* published toward the end of the nineteenth
century, James Bryce entitled one of his chapters "Why Great Men Are
Not Chosen President." With some notable exceptions, the Presidents
during the era he was discussing were a mediocre lot selected for reasons
that had nothing to do with their capacity to fill the office with distinction. During the bitter controversy over slavery, for example, both parties
sought innocuous candidates who could be depended upon to dodge the
issue. In 1840 the Whigs turned away from men of towering stature like
Henry Clay and Daniel Webster in favor of a relative nonentity like
William Henry Harrison. . . .

About fifty years later, when the nation was racked by agrarian dis-
content and the social consequences of urbanization and industrializa-
tion, the political parties still selected their candidates for partisan rather
than national reasons. In 1888, the Republican bosses, after a hectic
weekend of intrigues and bargaining, finally settled on the colorless
Benjamin Harrison, a "favorite son" of Indiana. Harrison's assets were
a brief term in the Senate, he had no scandals to hide, he came from a
doubtful state which might be won by his candidacy, was the grandson
of a President, and would offer no complications on the vital tariff
issue. A contemporary observer, commenting on the political conventions of the time, declared that they functioned like "the exquisite economy of Nature, which ever strives to get into each place the smallest man
that can fill it."

Nevertheless, feeble as the leadership frequently was, the Republic
prospered—the nation could afford the luxury of mediocrity. In our era,
however, when the President plays so strategic a role in promoting the
nation's welfare at home and safeguarding its position of world leadership abroad, a Grant or Harding in the White House would be an un-
mitigated disaster. Today his preparation must be such as to fully pre-

pare him to cope with the unprecedented problems not only at home but throughout the world.

Yet no school exists to train an aspirant for the unique and complex roles the Chief Executive is required to fill. Years spent in public service, whether in Congress, administration, or a governorship, may be helpful but do not necessarily prepare a man for greatness, or even for competence. If the Presidential office were merely administrative, involving technical proficiency in details and procedure, the requisite skills could be acquired. But, as Franklin D. Roosevelt once said, the Presidency is pre-eminently a place of moral leadership. What is therefore required is the ability to adapt the national purpose to the continually changing requirements of a dynamic society, to preserve and transmit to posterity the nation's heritage of humane and liberal values.

An impressive record of administrative competency may be misleading when assessing the potential of a candidate, as William Howard Taft sadly illustrates. Taft's distinguished career as judge, Governor-General of the Philippine Islands, and Secretary of War greatly impressed the party leaders. The judicial mind, however, is likely to hobble rather than to encourage vigorous executive leadership. In a crisis, the President must often rely on his instincts and intuition. If he stops too long to prepare an opinion by chewing over evidence and consulting precedents, the race may be finished before he enters the lists. Moreover, emphasis on the machinery of government and official routine can thwart the kind of initiative that thrusts a country forward. Franklin D. Roosevelt, who lacked both interest in and talent for routine administration, injected vitality into the councils of government.

A professional career in politics or a record of achievement in Congress is not necessarily a factor in the preparation of a President. Abraham Lincoln's experience on the national level was confined to a single term as a member of the House of Representatives a dozen years before his election as President. Woodrow Wilson spent a lifetime in the academic world and had only two years as governor of New Jersey before entering the White House, yet he exercised a vigorous, commanding leadership of Congress, scoring triumphs that seasoned politicians could envy. Even before the electorate had digested the significance of Wilson's "New Freedom," with its tariff reform, Federal Reserve Law, and Clayton antitrust legislation, it concluded that the scholar-turned-politician had proved a consummate master in the great game of politics. The failure that climaxed Wilson's administration was not caused by his lack of political experience, but was the result of a tragic flaw of personality.

By contrast, Calvin Coolidge was hardly an amateur in politics. He reached the heights of political power after serving as city councilman, a member of both houses of the state legislature, mayor, lieutenant-governor, governor, and Vice President. Yet during his six years in the White House, he offered the American people a steady stream of platitudes and banalities, encouraging a perilous blindness to the stirrings at home and abroad that were portents of debacle. As his biographer said, Coolidge believed his task was "to keep the Ship of State on an even keel before a favoring wind—not to reconstruct the hull or install motive power or alter the course. . . . He won no battles, challenged no traditions, instituted few reforms." Coolidge was completely inept as a party leader and a legislative leader. His bills were defeated and his vetoes overridden by Congress.

Whether a President will have the capacity to meet the demands made upon him by crises cannot be predicted solely on the basis of past achievement and service. If judged in terms of his background, James Buchanan should have been ideally suited for effective Presidential leadership. Few men came to office with a longer official training—forty years in the legislative, executive, and diplomatic service. Yet at a critical juncture in the nation's history, with the Union on a disaster course toward dissolution, he was tragically indecisive when the imperatives of the hour called for vigor and resolution.

Although Harry S Truman had been in political life for a fairly substantial period, his nomination for the Vice Presidency in 1944 was agreed to by Democratic party leaders mainly because he was an ideal compromise candidate—he was acceptable to both North and South, to organized labor, and to the machine bosses. No premature termination of Roosevelt's leadership was anticipated, and when it occurred the nation as a whole was appalled that its fate during such a precarious period was in the hands of this unassuming man. One journalist characterized the new President as "a sedative in a double-breasted suit," and most informed observers were prepared to write off his administration. Truman had not been a member of the inner war council or made privy to the negotiations at the various wartime conferences, or been informed about the progress of atomic development. But the years that followed were decision-packed, with Truman demonstrating an approach to foreign relations as unexpected as it was creative and imaginative.

To a great extent the Cabinet or parliamentary form of government in Great Britain solves the problem of unpredictability. The Prime Minister is the product of the House of Commons, steeped in its traditions and habituated to its ways, and he is required to have been the leader of his party in that body before he can be chosen the Queen's First Minister. . . . As head of his party, he has been displaying leadership for years in the law-making body of a kind that the electorate has endorsed. There are no "Johnny-come-latelys" or dark horses. By contrast, the President's preparation is largely a random affair. Still, ours is a Presidential system, and, that being so, what are the criteria that ultimately determine Presidential success if the traditional yardsticks are largely irrelevant? Is there a common pattern displayed by "strong" Presidents that might provide clues to whether a candidate is adequately prepared?

Perhaps most important is a broad, expansive view of the office that would permit the occupant of the White House to extend . . . executive prerogative to its outermost limits whenever the public necessity requires it. Theodore Roosevelt was better prepared for leadership by virtue of his approach to the Presidency than he was by the years he spent as police commissioner of New York, member of the federal Civil Service Commission, Assistant Secretary of the Navy, governor of New York, or even Vice President. As he once said: "The most important factor in getting the right spirit in my administration was my insistence upon the theory that the executive power was limited only by specific restrictions and prohibitions appearing in the Constitution or imposed by Congress under its constitutional power. . . . I declined to adopt the view that what was imperatively necessary for the nation could not be done by the President unless he could find some specific authorization to do it."

John Fitzgerald Kennedy regarded the Presidency as the repository of political and moral leadership, believing that the occupant of the office must be willing to use the powerful tools available to him. The choice, he felt, was to emulate either Roosevelt and Wilson or Taft and Harding. In an address before the National Press Club a year before his inauguration he left no room for doubt as to which of the Presidents he would use as models. "Whatever the political affiliations of our next President," he said, "whatever his views may be on all the issues and problems that rush in upon us, he must above all be the Chief Executive in every sense of the word. He must be prepared to exercise the fullest powers of his office, all that are specified and some that are not. He must master complex problems as well as receive one-page memoranda. He must originate action as well as study groups. He must reopen the channels of communication between the world of thought and the seat of power."

It is no coincidence that throughout our history the Presidents who have been most ineffectual were those like Taylor, Taft, Harding, and Coolidge, who were firmly committed to the concept that the Chief Executive could exercise only that authority specifically granted him by the Constitution. Taft could be considered their spokesman with his declaration that "the President can exercise no power which cannot be fairly and reasonably traced to some specific grant of power or justly implied and included within such express grant as proper and necessary to its exercise."

However rich and varied the candidate's career, he comes ill-prepared to discharge the duties and responsibilities of the Presidential office if his theoretical position would inhibit rather than encourage bold, assertive leadership. In less tempestuous and complex times this element in the preparation of a President was of no great significance. As a matter of fact, the relatively untroubled periods in our history produced the textbook image of the Presidency as an equal and coordinate branch operating strictly within its own sphere and never trespassing beyond certain specified boundary lines. Today, however, it must encompass party and legislative leadership, providing direction in economic matters and initiative in world affairs.

Significantly, with the exception of George Washington, all the Presidents who made a lasting impact on the nation were men who eagerly sought the office and were avid for leadership in public affairs. To reach the White House would be to fulfill their profoundest ambitions. Once in office, they approached their tasks with driving zest and enthusiasm. Theodore Roosevelt, who was elevated to the Presidency through an accident of fate, probably would have achieved it eventually on his own. He reveled in the opportunity to occupy the seat of power. For him the Presidency was a glorious adventure and he enjoyed every minute of it; for his successor, whom he had hand-picked, it was an ordeal that he endured with outward stoicism but inward wretchedness. William Howard Taft was persuaded to take a job he never wanted and for which, realistically, he felt ill-suited. "Politics, when I am in it, makes me sick," he once said. His private letters offer pathetic evidence of his lack of self-confidence. Several months after his inauguration he wrote to Roosevelt:

If I followed my impulse, I should still say "My dear Mr. President." I cannot overcome the habit. When I am addressed as "Mr. President," I turn to see whether you are not at my elbow. . . .

I want you to know that I do nothing in the Executive Office without considering what you would do under the circumstances and without having in a sense a mental talk with you over the pros and cons of the situation. I have not the facility for educating the public as you had. . . .

The Presidency is a lonely place—that "splendid misery" as Thomas Jefferson once called it—especially in times of crisis when the occupant of the office must repeatedly make vital decisions for which he alone is responsible. No one can share the burden with him, and only a man who has confidence in his own judgment is adequately prepared for White House leadership. Harry S Truman's initial response to the news of President Roosevelt's sudden death was certainly understandable. "I don't know whether you fellows ever had a load of hay or a bull fall on you," he told reporters, "but last night the stars and all the planets fell on me. . . . I've got the most terribly responsible job any man ever had." But Truman's inner core was sound and firm. Within weeks he began to demonstrate the inner security that enabled him to deal with the many grave problems that beset the nation.

Woodrow Wilson's self-confidence was of another caliber. His lack of humility, tinged with mysticism was to prove his undoing. "God ordained that I should be the next President of the United States," he announced as he was about to enter the White House. On another occasion he said, "I am sorry for those who disagree with me because I know I am right." While the President must be firmly convinced that the course he has chosen *is* the right one, he must at the same time be flexible when circumstances require resilient behavior.

A significant element in a President's preparation is that he have a plan that embodies his view of the country's future. It should reflect his talent for creative innovation and demonstrate a sense of the direction in which the times are moving, diagnose contemporary maladies, and offer possible means for their solution. Today that plan must embrace Ghana and Ceylon as well as Georgia and Oregon. In Franklin D. Roosevelt's campaign speeches in 1932, he presented a plan for the economic future of the nation that was as bold in outline as it was imaginative. Although containing no specific blueprint, it articulated goals that were the basis for the "New Deal" program.

While campaign rhetoric and political oratory can be discounted to a large extent, they provide some means for discerning the quality of a candidate. What could have been expected from Warren G. Harding on the basis of the hackneyed speeches delivered from the front porch of his home? As William G. McAdoo colorfully put it, his addresses "leave the impression of an army of pompous phrases moving over the landscape in search of an idea; sometimes these meandering words would actually capture a straggling thought and bear it triumphantly, a prisoner in their midst, until it died of servitude and overwork!" The nation at the time was not aware of the machinations that gave Harding the nomination, but Americans recklessly voted for a man whose strangest claim to the highest office in the land was that he *looked* like a President.

A leading contemporary journal in all seriousness declared that whatever might be the defects of the nominee as a world statesman, Harding was "an exceedingly courteous gentleman." If he were elected, "good nature, both to political friends and to political enemies," would once again prevail in the White House. "The Senator's speeches may be properly criticized for their vagueness, for their lack of original thought, for their occasionally conflicting character . . . but they are certainly not lacking in the decencies of political controversy. And this is another case where style is the man."

Style is indeed the man. The last sentence, which succinctly and accurately summed up the matter, was a portent. The character of the nation is influenced by the "style" of its chosen head. With "normalcy" enthroned in the White House, the nation drifted, devitalized, without elevated standards or meritorious goals.

Leadership in our democratic society performs a strategic role above and beyond the functions mapped out by our constitutional system. An essential component is the President's capacity and will to influence public opinion so that necessary programs are carried out. Those men who were strong Presidents had both an intellectual and intuitive comprehension of this ingredient. As Theodore Roosevelt put it, "Our prime necessity is that public opinion should be properly educated." And again, "I do not desire to act unless I can get the bulk of our people to understand the situation and to back up the action; and to do that I have to get the facts vividly before them." The ineffectual Presidents were either indifferent about shaping public opinion or believed, with Calvin Coolidge, that "the people have their own affairs to look after and cannot give much attention to what Congress is doing."

The preparation of a President, then, is compounded of many intangibles. Attributes for which there is no specific training—character, convictions, and style—appear to be more basic for successful leadership than background, training, and experience. Political skill taken for granted, the effective leader captures the public imagination because he possesses moral and physical stamina, because he has a humanitarian outlook and the determination to alleviate the ills that plague our society, and because when he speaks and acts he does so not only for the moment but for the age. He has the capacity to inspire the people, to elevate them above the commonplace, to set a tone for the nation so that the vision of the future becomes the objective for the present. Such a President is a total President, both a politician and a statesman.

part four

ROLES AND FUNCTIONS

I

Chief Executive

Article II of the Constitution begins, "The executive power shall be vested in a President of the United States of America," and Section 3 requires him to see that the laws are faithfully executed. These provisions, coupled with his responsibility as the head of a vast bureaucracy, represent the essential elements in the President's role as Chief Executive.

The opening sentence of Article II has provoked lively controversy among commentators on the Constitution, and has been differently interpreted by different occupants of the White House. Advocates of an enlarged view of presidential prerogative contend that the "executive power" phrase in the opening clause invests the Chief Executive with broad, inherent powers apart from those specifically enumerated in later sections of the Article. Those who favor a restricted view argue that an undefined plenitude of authority would threaten the constitutional principle of the separation of powers.

Constitutional safeguards and the national tradition, however, virtually rule out the possibility of a dangerous usurpation of power by the Chief Executive. Not only the governmental structure with its Supreme Court and Congress, but various elements in the political process—powerful interest groups, public opinion, and entrenched sectors of the executive bureaucracy—would deter even the boldest President from attempting such an effort. At the same time, it is incumbent on the highest elected official in the nation to employ every available means to implement his policies, and see to it that legislative enactments are enforced and judicial decisions carried out.

Federal Troops Sent to Little Rock, Arkansas, 1957

When a Federal Court order, which directed the Little Rock, Arkansas, school system to desegregate, was defied by the state government, President Eisenhower dispatched federal troops to the city to enforce the decree. In a radio and television address to the American people, that

Public Papers of the Presidents of the United States, Dwight D. Eisenhower, 1957 (Washington, D.C.: U.S. Government Printing Office, 1958), pp. 689-694.

same day, the President spoke about the necessity to enforce the laws,
and he declared that a failure to act in the face of mob violence would
ultimately lead to anarchy and a breakdown of the American system of law.

Good Evening, My Fellow Citizens:

FOR A FEW minutes this evening I want to speak to you about the serious situation that has arisen in Little Rock. To make this talk I have come to the President's office in the White House. I could have spoken from Rhode Island, where I have been staying recently, but I felt that, in speaking from the house of Lincoln, of Jackson and of Wilson, my words would better convey both the sadness I feel in the action I was compelled today to take and the firmness with which I intend to pursue this course until the orders of the Federal Court at Little Rock can be executed without unlawful interference.

In that city, under the leadership of demagogic extremists, disorderly mobs have deliberately prevented the carrying out of proper orders from a Federal Court. Local authorities have not eliminated that violent opposition and, under the law, I yesterday issued a Proclamation calling upon the mob to disperse.

This morning the mob again gathered in front of the Central High School of Little Rock, obviously for the purpose of again preventing the carrying out of the Court's order relating to the admission of Negro children to that school.

Whenever normal agencies prove inadequate to the task and it becomes necessary for the Executive Branch of the Federal Government to use its powers and authority to uphold Federal Courts, the President's responsibility is inescapable.

In accordance with that responsibility, I have today issued an Executive Order directing the use of troops under Federal authority to aid in the execution of Federal law at Little Rock, Arkansas. This became necessary when my Proclamation of yesterday was not observed, and the obstruction of justice still continues.

It is important that the reasons for my action be understood by all our citizens.

As you know, the Supreme Court of the United States has decided that separate public educational facilities for the races are inherently unequal and therefore compulsory school segregation laws are unconstitutional.

Our personal opinions about the decision have no bearing on the matter of enforcement; the responsibility and authority of the Supreme Court to interpret the Constitution are very clear. Local Federal Courts were instructed by the Supreme Court to issue such orders and decrees as might be necessary to achieve admission to public schools without regard to race—and with all deliberate speed.

During the past several years, many communities in our Southern States have instituted public school plans for gradual progress in the enrollment and attendance of school children of all races in order to bring themselves into compliance with the law of the land.

They thus demonstrated to the world that we are a nation in which laws, not men, are supreme.

I regret to say that this truth—the cornerstone of our liberties—was not observed in this instance.

It was my hope that this localized situation would be brought under control by city and State authorities. If the use of local police powers had been sufficient, our traditional method of leaving the problems in those hands would have been pursued. But when large gatherings of obstructionists made it impossible for the decrees of the Court to be carried out, both the law and the national interest demanded that the President take action.

Here is the sequence of events in the development of the Little Rock school case.

In May of 1955, the Little Rock School Board approved a moderate plan for the gradual desegregation of the public schools in that city. It provided that a start toward integration would be made at the present term in the high school, and that the plan would be in full operation by 1963. Here I might say that in a number of communities in Arkansas integration in the schools has already started and without violence of any kind. Now this Little Rock plan was challenged in the courts by some who believed that the period of time as proposed in the plan was too long.

The United States Court at Little Rock, which has supervisory responsibility under the law for the plan of desegregation in the public schools, dismissed the challenge, thus approving a gradual rather than an abrupt change from the existing system. The court found that the school board had acted in good faith in planning for a public school system free from racial discrimination.

Since that time, the court has on three separate occasions issued orders directing that the plan be carried out. All persons were instructed to refrain from interfering with the efforts of the school board to comply with the law.

Proper and sensible observance of the law then demanded the respectful obedience which the nation has a right to expect from all its people. This, unfortunately, has not been the case at Little Rock. Certain misguided persons, many of them imported into Little Rock by agitators, have insisted upon defying the law and have sought to bring it into disrepute. The orders of the court have thus been frustrated.

The very basis of our individual rights and freedoms rests upon the certainty that the President and the Executive Branch of Government will support and insure the carrying out of the decisions of the Federal Courts, even, when necessary with all the means at the President's command.

Unless the President did so, anarchy would result.

There would be no security for any except that which each one of us could provide for himself.

The interest of the nation in the proper fulfillment of the law's requirements cannot yield to opposition and demonstrations by some few persons.

Mob rule cannot be allowed to override the decisions of our courts.

Now, let me make it very clear that Federal troops are not being used to relieve local and state authorities of their primary duty to preserve the peace and order of the community. Nor are the troops there for the purpose of taking over the responsibility of the School Board and the other responsible local officials in running Central High School. The running of our school system and the maintenance of peace and order in each of our States are strictly local affairs and the Federal Government does not interfere except in a very few special cases and when requested by one of the several States. In the present case the troops are there, pursuant to law, solely for the purpose of preventing interference with the orders of the Court.

The proper use of the powers of the Executive Branch to enforce the orders of a Federal Court is limited to extraordinary and compelling circumstances. Manifestly, such an extreme situation has been created in Little Rock. This challenge must be met and with such measures as will preserve to the people as a whole their lawfully-protected rights in a climate permitting their free and fair exercise.

The overwhelming majority of our people in every section of the country are united in their respect for observance of the law—even in those cases where they may disagree with that law.

They deplore the call of extremists to violence.

The decision of the Supreme Court concerning school integration, of course, affects the South more seriously than it does other sections of the country. In that region I have many warm friends, some of them in the city of Little Rock. I have deemed it a great personal privilege to spend in our Southland tours of duty while in the military service and enjoyable recreational periods since that time.

So from intimate personal knowledge, I know that the overwhelming majority of the people in the South—including those of Arkansas and of Little Rock—are of good will, united in their efforts to preserve and respect the law even when they disagree with it.

They do not sympathize with mob rule. They, like the rest of our nation, have proved in two great wars their readiness to sacrifice for America.

A foundation of our American way of life is our national respect for law.

In the South, as elsewhere, citizens are keenly aware of the tremendous disservice that has been done to the people of Arkansas in the eyes of the nation, and that has been done to the nation in the eyes of the world.

At a time when we face grave situations abroad because of the hatred that Communism bears toward a system of government based on human rights, it would be difficult to exaggerate the harm that is being done to the prestige and influence, and indeed to the safety, of our nation and the world.

Our enemies are gloating over this incident and using it everywhere to misrepresent our whole nation. We are portrayed as a violator of those standards of conduct which the peoples of the world united to proclaim in the Charter of the United Nations. There they affirmed "faith in fundamental human rights" and "in the dignity and worth of the human person" and they did so "without distinction as to race, sex, language or religion."

And so, with deep confidence, I call upon the citizens of the State of Arkansas to assist in bringing to an immediate end all interference with the law and its processes. If resistance to the Federal Court orders ceases at once, the further presence of Federal troops will be unnecessary and the city of Little Rock will return to its normal habits of peace and order and a blot upon the fair name and high honor of our nation in the world will be removed.

Thus will be restored the image of America and of all its parts as one nation, indivisible, with liberty and justice for all.

Good night, and thank you very much.

NOTE: The President referred to Proclamation 3204 "Obstruction of Justice in the State of Arkansas" and Executive Order 10730 "Providing Assistance for the Removal of an Obstruction of Justice Within the State of Arkansas," published in the Federal Register (22 F.R. 7628) and in Title 3 of the Code of Federal Regulations.

2

Chief Legislator

The Constitution involves the President in numerous aspects of the legislative process. He is required to report to Congress on the state of the Union; his approval is necessary before bills can become law; and he may call Congress into special session. To these duties the strong Presidents of the modern era have added a new dimension of leadership: the initiation of legislative measures and the responsibility for their passage through all stages of the law-making process.

A President's perspective, like that of a Congressman, is influenced by the nature of his constituency. Elected by the nation at large, he feels it incumbent to propose or support programs vital to the interests of the majority of Americans, who are concentrated in the urban and industrial sections of the country. Since the members of Congress are subject to particularistic pressures, the President is frequently obliged to battle for his legislation. To win his objective, the strong President employs every legitimate tool at his command, not only those granted him by the Constitution, but also devices such as patronage, the appeal to public opinion, and even coercion.

Because the President has to deal with a legislative body fragmented by independent centers of power and lacking in party discipline and cohesion, only assertive leadership can elicit from Congress the effort necessary to fulfill popular needs.

Relations Between the White House and Capitol Hill

Lawrence F. O'Brien, a special assistant to the President for congressional affairs in the Kennedy and Johnson administrations (until his appointment as Postmaster-General), has described in a television interview the means employed by the White House to attain its legislative program. He provides some valuable insights into the detailed planning and organization required to develop an effective relationship with Congress.

Transcript of the interview broadcast by National Educational Television the week of July 11, 1965, on a show titled "From the White House to the Hill," as part of its series on "The Changing Congress." Congressional Quarterly Weekly Report, XXIII, No. 30 (July 23, 1965), pp. 1434-1436. Reprinted by permission.

Q. (MR. PAUL DUKA, National Broadcasting Company) Larry, how do you see the function and scope of the White House liaison?

A. (Mr. O'Brien) Well, it's certainly developed into an important element, the operation of the White House, when you think back on the history of Congressional relations, the fact that to some extent it was not only non-existent White House-to-the-Hill in the days of Wilson and through a period following President Wilson we had the situation of no rapport between the two branches of Government. They seemed to be at cross purposes, and in the era of Roosevelt, the first hundred days, of course, a massive legislative program was enacted. The situation at the moment called for it, and following that, however, after the so-called "court-packing" period, there was a slackening off again in this area. I think this went on to a considerable extent until a point in the Eisenhower Administration, where it was, if you will, reformalized and put on a departmental level in the White House.

With us, of course, it was the problem that we were faced with after the 1960 election, while we had secured the White House; nevertheless, we lost 21 seats. Solid, voting Democrats had been defeated in the '60 election, and it was immediately apparent that we were going to have great difficulties. So we had to take a very close look at the type of operation we might put into effect, and what procedures we could follow. We were hard put to it—the realities of the situation were that the New Frontier Program was massive, and we were in a tight bind in the Congress, particularly in the House.

So my view now in the fifth legislative year I've been in the White House is that it has been awfully productive to us. It really made an impact on the program, and I think finally it has been determined that within the constitutional limitations, it is feasible and proper to have a close rapport with the Legislative Branch of Government; that this doesn't in any sense violate the constitutional provisions or the historic concept, if you will, of the relationship of the two branches. It's just the human element is present, as it is in all activities in life, and the closer the relationship, the better the understanding, the greater the possibilities of ultimate enactment of the White House proposals.

After all, we recognize that the President proposes, and it is up to the Legislative Branch of the Government to dispose. But certainly there is no known barrier to constantly advocating our program . . . to the people and to the Congress.

So I would have to say that in retrospect—viewing the situation in January '61 and thinking back today to that period—that obviously there has been real progress. I don't think perhaps there's been a five year period in our history similar to the five years here in the White House in this Democratic Administration. I think not only in the number of legislative proposals that have been enacted, but when you look at the substance of these proposals, the far-reaching impact of many of the bills that have been enacted during the period—hopefully will be enacted before this session comes to an end—it all points to a permanency, I think, in relationships of this nature. It is a department of the White House, it involves a variety of individual contact with Members of Congress, and I must say it's developed into a two-way street up and down Pennsylvania Avenue. There's not any hesitancy I'm able to observe on the part of the Member of House or Senate to contact the White House to discuss matters of mutual interest, nor is there any hesitancy on our part to do the same. And as far as I can determine, it's worked out quite well.

Q. You mentioned the formalization of the liaison office under President Kennedy. I think it's quite true. How did he come to do this? How did he come to set up a liaison chief with one man delegated for the House and one man deleted for the Senate under you? Were there any recommendations for this . . . any studies made that this would be a feasible thing to do?

A. There were discussions involving Professor Dick Neustadt and others. I think, however, that the President's judgment to a great extent, as I indicated, was based, if you will, on the political reality of the situation when we moved into this building—that we had a difficult situation ahead of us and just what conceivably could be done about it. And I recall President Kennedy at one time saying to me, "I see a great deal— Members of Congress individually and in groups—we seem to have a great deal of contact with them"; and he said, "I recall my fourteen years on the Hill, and I cannot recall during that fourteen-year period having any direct or meaningful contact with a Member of the White House staff."

Now, when you think about it for a moment, his years on the Hill were split between the House and the Senate—I believe six and eight. And I can see how that would occur, that in that period the concentration contact-wise was pretty much confined to the top leadership, and the average Member, if you will, seniority-wise, probably wasn't exposed to any great extent to this type of contact. And I think it struck President Kennedy that on this end of the Avenue he found that this was a meaningful, daily activity. And when you looked at the statistics of contact and realize the extent of this activity, I imagine he thought back to his years on the Hill and wondered just what took place during those years.

But I think if he had been a committee chairman, or had, say, fourteen years plus seniority in one body, perhaps he would have been exposed to the White House contact. But that wasn't the case, at least, as he remembered the years, and it intrigued him. And then furthermore, it was, as we have said, rather informal, and it was not departmentalized and placed on the level operationally that it has been placed over the last five years.

And again I feel that there are pluses and minuses in the views of observers, some political scientists and others in this activity, but we feel the pluses far outweigh the minuses that conceivably could be conjured up. And I therefore think that as the years go on, this type of contact and relationship will continue—perhaps be further refined—but I think it's here to stay now. It represents an historic breakthrough in this relationship.

Q. Well, with a limited staff and more than 500 members, how can you keep up with your job?

A. Well, that entered our minds when we started this operation, but of course there are Congressional liaison chiefs in each department and agency of the Government. Our feeling was that we had to unify this activity, we had to centralize it in the sense that it would be a team effort, and we inaugurated a new procedure. And that is that each department and agency would provide to us by Monday noon of each week a written report of the department's activity with the Congress over the prior week and the projection for the current week.

Now, we take those reports and review them on Monday afternoon and present an analysis to the President for his night reading on Monday, along with a suggested agenda for his use, if he so desires, of the leadership meetings that are held on Tuesday mornings.

In addition, we have these Congressional relations people—there are about forty of them—they're in these key roles in departments and agencies—in periodically to the White House to discuss our mutual legislative problems. And the emphasis constantly is on the President's program, that all elements of this program really in the final analysis are part of a single program, that the downtown in this building . . . the only man I'm aware of who's been elected to office is the President of the United States. And he has proposed to the people what he conceives his program to be. The people made a determination that he should be their President. Furthermore, you have the Democratic Party Platform, and it is, as we see it, a mandate for action.

So by establishing this team and working very, very closely with these people in the departments and agencies, it gave us additional manpower, and it insured that our activities would be properly channeled for maximum results, and we would not have cross-wires and individuals going off in separate directions and working with the Congress.

Now, President Johnson has emphasized and re-emphasized this, as you know, and on many occasions at Cabinet meetings he re-states his concern about the progress of his program, the Great Society program: his intention that every member of the Executive Branch be involved, the responsibility of the Cabinet member in this area. He has stated to them on several occasions in my presence that no person in his respective department could ever be any more important than the head of the Congressional relations activity. And he places the responsibility directly on the Cabinet member in that regard.

So there is a total awareness that we've developed over these years that as I said is re-emphasized constantly by President Johnson—awareness that this team effort is a continuing, day in and day out effort.

For example, we would anticipate that the Secretary of Agriculture would have a great interest in our education program, although it does not come directly under his activities in his department. Nevertheless, he has friends and associates on the Hill, and he would be an advocate of our educational legislation whenever an opportunity presented itself. And likewise across the board the entire program.

And in addition to that, even here on the White House staff, the special assistants to the President who are working in other areas are under Presidential direction always available to us for assistance and support as we move along through the legislative year. Nothing has a greater priority in the President's view than the legislative program, and I think when you look at the program and analyze it, you can understand that, because we are at this moment engaged in most meaningful legislative activity, again in the field of education—with all the progress that we have made, with the great elementary-secondary education bill that was enacted earlier this year. We still have additional proposals in this area. There will always be an unfinished agenda.

We are still working on our "medicare" program, and our voting rights legislation. And we have several meaningful proposals in the field of health and research. And all of this is so important that you have to bring into focus every element of potential that you can possibly bring in to help promote the program.

Now, they talk about arm twisting and all that sort of thing. And I read these stories with great interest, because this just does not exist. The fact of the matter is that what we have by way of strength, if we do have anything in promoting the program, is the attitude of the average member of Congress toward the President. This has applied to President Kennedy, and it applies to President Johnson, that there is a good feeling on the Hill, if you will, toward the President. There is a realization of his massive problems, there is an attitude of general acceptance of his basic proposals in the legislative area, and therefore we find that doors are open to us. The members are interested in hearing our views, we are equally interested in having their views, and their views are extremely important.

So I think that basically is what you have going for you, to use the vernacular. This suggestion that you trade the bridge or the dam or some project for a vote, and that sort of thing, well, it's just not the case.

I think that we can continue to make progress in this area and our relationships with the Congress if we never lose sight of one important factor (the fellows on the staff here remind themselves constantly of this, and all those in key roles in the Executive Branch remind themselves constantly) that there are on the Hill 535 *elected* officials. They have been elected by the people; they have been in the ballot box, so to speak, and we must recognize this. All of us are appointed, and in our form of government we must constantly be aware of the role of the elected office holder, appreciate his problems, understand his responsibilities. And as long as we continue to have that clearly in mind, we're in no position, nor should we be, nor would we want to be, to dictate in any sense— that this is a matter of firm belief in a program that affects all of America—and that belief in this program is shared generally on the Hill. Individual members have individual views relating to various aspects of the program, but we can work together, and again, we can only propose and advocate. The decision is made on the other end of Pennsylvania Avenue, and we recognize and respect it. . . .

Q. Why is the Administration's help needed to get most major legislation through these days?

A. Why, I think that over this five years you have to go back again to a strong President who exerts leadership, who was willing to step out and propose, who was willing to put the weight of his office behind the proposals, who was at all times attempting to encourage the average citizen to join with him. All of this places you, I think, in a much stronger position, because with—the President, after all, gets the attention of the people to a far greater extent than any other leader, and they are interested in his views. They will listen to him. He commands massive audiences on television and radio, and public appearances. And I think that it's an important element in legislative success, the success of the program, to have a President not only advocating initially, but constantly reminding, if you will, everyone of the program and its meaning, and giving proof positive that he is not only proposing, but he is vitally concerned personally.

And that transmits to the public, and in turn, from our point of view, is helpful to us on the Hill, because we have to anticipate that these Members, as I've said before, elected to office, are going to react to the views of their constituency. And that's in the nature of things the way it should be, and we can only hope the constituency view transmitted to them by letter and personal contact will be more often than not our view, and therefore becomes everyone's view.

I think the difference between initiating on the Hill and initiating here is obvious, because the initiation by the President makes for greater impact, greater citizen interest, and consequently, I think ultimately, closer attention on the Hill. . . .

3

Commander-in-Chief

In assigning the role of commander-in-chief to the President, the framers of the Constitution ensured civilian supremacy over the military. And by delegating to Congress the power to declare war, they expected that in this area, too, their elaborate system of checks and balances would operate. The first feature is still maintained, but circumstances have practically nullified the latter.

President Polk's orders to General Taylor in 1846, directing him to occupy disputed territory below the Rio Grande River, resulted in a clash with Mexican troops in which a number of American soldiers were killed. Immediately the President asked Congress to issue a declaration of war. At this point, the legislative body had no choice but to formalize an already existing situation, which presidential initiative had created.

The nature of America's place in the twentieth-century world is such that the President, in order to carry out global commitments or for other reasons, can more easily involve the nation in armed hostilities. The Korean conflict was designated a "police action," but despite this euphemism, it was a large scale war which Congress never authorized. Nevertheless, the legislature has endeavored to maintain its constitutional prerogative. In 1951 the Senate clashed, in one of its periodic "great debates," over the right of the President to dispatch troops to Europe in peacetime in fulfillment of the nation's obligations under the North Atlantic Treaty. The point at issue was whether Congress would not then be surrendering its lawful authority. Considering the times, an outcome favorable to the President was almost a foregone conclusion.

In an era of intercontinental ballistic missiles, decision-making has gravitated to the one office which can act with speed and secrecy. The President continues to consult with Congress or to seek its support through resolutions, but in crises—such as the missile confrontation in Cuba with the Soviet Union, or the Vietnam situation—the President can bring the nation to the verge of war or even into war. When he decides to act on his belief that the nation's security is imperiled, neither the Senate Foreign Relations Committee, nor the Congress as a whole, nor even public opinion can halt the momentum generated by the White House.

The Dismissal of General Douglas MacArthur

Although appointments to high military rank are subject to approval by the Senate, the power of the President as commander-in-chief to discharge such appointees is unchallenged. President Lincoln removed General McClellan when he felt that his performance was unsatisfactory. Similarly, President Truman removed General MacArthur, a brilliant military commander acclaimed as a wartime hero, because the strategy he publicly recommended for fighting the Korean War was in direct opposition to that advocated by the Joint Chiefs of Staff. Moreover, MacArthur's statements had political implications at variance with the policy to which the government was committed of a limited war for limited objectives.

ORDER TO GENERAL MACARTHUR FROM THE PRESIDENT

I DEEPLY REGRET that it becomes my duty as President and Commander in Chief of the United States military forces to replace you as Supreme Commander, Allied Powers; Commander in Chief, United Nations Com-

Congressional Record, 82nd Congress, 1st Session (April 10, 1951), pp. 3179-3180.

mand; Commander in Chief, Far East; and Commanding General, U. S. Army, Far East.

You will turn over your commands, effective at once, to Lt. Gen. Matthew B. Ridgway. You are authorized to have issued such orders as are necessary to complete desired travel to such place as you select.

My reasons for your replacement will be made public concurrently with the delivery to you of the foregoing order, and are contained in the next following message. (See attached statement by the President.)

STATEMENT BY THE PRESIDENT

With deep regret I have concluded that General of the Army Douglas MacArthur is unable to give his wholehearted support to the policies of the United States Government and of the United Nations in matters pertaining to his official duties. In view of the specific responsibilities imposed upon me by the Constitution of the United States and the added responsibility which has been entrusted to me by the United Nations, I have decided that I must make a change of command in the Far East. I have, therefore, relieved General MacArthur of his commands and have designated Lt. Gen. Matthew B. Ridgway as his successor.

Full and vigorous debate on matters of national policy is a vital element in the constitutional system of our free democracy. It is fundamental, however, that military commanders must be governed by the policies and directives issued to them in the manner provided by our laws and Constitution. In time of crisis, this consideration is particularly compelling.

General MacArthur's place in history as one of our greatest commanders is fully established. The Nation owes him a debt of gratitude for the distinguished and exceptional service which he has rendered his country in posts of great responsibility. For that reason I repeat my regret at the necessity for the action I feel compelled to take in his case.

President Kennedy's Quarantine of Cuba

When unassailable evidence reached the White House in October 1962, that the Russians were arming Cuba with intermediate range ballistic

Public Papers of the Presidents of the United States, John F. Kennedy, 1962 (Washington, D.C.: U.S. Government Printing Office, 1963), pp. 809-811.

missiles—despite their denials that they were supplying the country with "offensive weapons"—President Kennedy acted promptly. In a public statement he denounced the Soviet action, declaring that he intended to eliminate the missile bases with every means at his disposal, beginning with a "quarantine" of all ships carrying military equipment into Cuba.

When the Strategic Air Command was alerted and troops mobilized in Florida for a possible invasion, the world literally held its breath for a week. At the same time, while a Soviet response was awaited, the President employed the utmost tact and diplomacy to enable a Russian withdrawal from the situation without a loss of "face." The episode illustrates the awesome uses to which the President's power as commander-in-chief can be put.

By the President of the United States of America a Proclamation:

WHEREAS THE PEACE of the world and the security of the United States and of all American States are endangered by reason of the establishment by the Sino-Soviet powers of an offensive military capability in Cuba, including bases for ballistic missiles with a potential range covering most of North and South America;

Whereas by a Joint Resolution passed by the Congress of the United States and approved on October 3, 1962, it was declared that the United States is determined to prevent by whatever means may be necessary, including the use of arms, the Marxist-Leninist regime in Cuba from extending, by force or the threat of force, its aggressive or subversive activities to any part of this hemisphere, and to prevent in Cuba the creation or use of an externally supported military capability endangering the security of the United States; and

Whereas the Organ of Consultation of the American Republics meeting in Washington on October 23, 1962, recommended that the Member States, in accordance with Articles 6 and 8 of the Inter-American Treaty of Reciprocal Assistance, take all measures, individually and collectively, including the use of armed force, which they may deem necessary to ensure that the Government of Cuba cannot continue to receive from the Sino-Soviet powers military material and related supplies which may threaten the peace and security of the Continent and to prevent the missiles in Cuba with offensive capability from ever becoming an active threat to the peace and security of the Continent:

Now, Therefore, I, John F. Kennedy, President of the United States of America, acting under and by virtue of the authority conferred upon me by the Constitution and statutes of the United States, in accordance with the aforementioned resolutions of the United States Congress and of the Organ of Consultation of the American Republics, and to defend the security of the United States, do hereby proclaim that the forces under my command are ordered, beginning at 2:00 p.m. Greenwich time October 24, 1962, to interdict, subject to the instructions herein contained, the delivery of offensive weapons and associated material to Cuba.

For the purposes of this Proclamation, the following are declared to be prohibited materiel:

Surface-to-surface missiles; bomber aircraft; bombs; air-to-surface rockets and guided missiles; warheads for any of the above weapons; mechanical or electronic equipment to support or operate the above items; and any other classes of materiel hereafter designated by the Secretary of Defense for the purpose of effectuating this Proclamation.

To enforce this order, the Secretary of Defense shall take appropriate measures to prevent the delivery of prohibited materiel to Cuba, employing the land, sea and air forces of the United States in cooperation with any forces that may be made available by other American States.

The Secretary of Defense may make such regulations and issue such directives as he deems necessary to ensure the effectiveness of this order, including the designation, within a reasonable distance of Cuba, of prohibited or restricted zones and of prescribed routes.

Any vessel or craft which may be proceeding toward Cuba may be intercepted and may be directed to identify itself, its cargo, equipment and stores and its ports of call, to stop, to lie to, to submit to visit and search, or to proceed as directed. Any vessel or craft which fails or refuses to respond to or comply with directions shall be subject to being taken into custody. Any vessel or craft which it is believed is en route to Cuba and may be carrying prohibited materiel or may itself constitute such materiel shall, wherever possible, be directed to proceed to another destination of its own choice and shall be taken into custody if it fails or refuses to obey such directions. All vessels or craft taken into custody shall be sent into a port of the United States for appropriate disposition.

In carrying out this order, force shall not be used except in case of failure or refusal to comply with directions, or with regulations or directives of the Secretary of Defense issued hereunder, after reasonable efforts have been made to communicate them to the vessel or craft, or in the case of self-defense. In any case, force shall be used only to the extent necessary.

In Witness Whereof, I have hereunto set my hand and cause the seal of the United States of America to be affixed.

Done in the City of Washington this twenty-third day of October in the year of our Lord nineteen hundred and sixty-two, and of [SEAL] the Independence of the United States of America the one hundred and eighty-seventh.

JOHN F. KENNEDY

By the President:
DEAN RUSK
Secretary of State

4

World Leader

The ultimate director of the nation's foreign relations, the President has always been, as the High Court once phrased it, the supreme organ of the nation in its foreign affairs. In the early years of the Republic, when disengagement from the interests and rivalries of foreign nations was the most appropriate policy to promote security and independence, the President was concerned for the most part with domestic affairs. With the emergence of the United States as a world power in the twentieth century, however, the Presidency has been elevated to a position of world importance and a new dimension has been added to presidential leadership.

Theodore Roosevelt foreshadowed the presidential role of world leader. Believing that a European balance of power was essential to American security, he used his personal influence and the prestige of his office to achieve a peaceful settlement of the Franco-German dispute over Morocco. Similarly, recognizing that the balance of power in the Far East had implications for American interests, he intervened in the Russo-Japanese war. Six decades and two world wars later, the Chief Executive presides over a nation which has military alliances and political commitments extending to all continents, which has bases and missile sites along the periphery of the entire Communist bloc, and which has a populace living constantly in the shadow (or center) of international crisis. *The President is involved with the entire world, for events however remote from the United States can affect its position in the power struggle and ideological contest with foreign adversaries.*

As a world leader, the President must address himself to varied "constituencies"—the people of his own nation, the people of the nations with which the United States is allied, the people of the nonaligned nations in Africa and Asia, the people of the Communist world, and the United Nations as a corporate body. The task of harmonizing all of these presents a formidable challenge to presidential leadership.

Recently the whole area of foreign policy has been affected by a factor of unparalleled and omnipresent significance—nuclear weaponry. The revolution in military technology, paradoxically, has made the President both more and less powerful in exercising his role as foreign policy maker. While he can order the deployment of the most destructive weapon in history, his freedom of action is circumscribed because if he behaves in as arbitrary a manner as some of his predecessors, he might unleash a nuclear holocaust.

The tremendous complication of world affairs and the enlarged responsibilities of the United States have resulted in an increasing institutionalization of the presidential function in foreign policy. A few important developments since World War II can be cited: the formation of the National Security Council to assist the President in coordinating military, diplomatic, and economic strategies; the designation of a special assistant to the President on national security affairs; the creation of the Central Intelligence Agency; and the bureaucratic proliferation within the Department of State.

The Truman Doctrine

In 1947, with Greece and Turkey on the verge of political and economic collapse, Great Britain announced that it could no longer meet its commitments in the Near East. A British withdrawal would have left the way open for Soviet expansion into the area. If Greece and Turkey had been drawn into the Communist orbit, Iran in all likelihood would have followed. Italy, with a large Communist party, would then have been subjected to Soviet pressure, and the security of all western Europe endangered.

Recognizing that only the United States was capable of halting Communist expansion, President Truman announced to a joint session

Public Papers of the Presidents of the United States, Harry S. Truman, 1947 (Washington, D.C.: U.S. Government Printing Office, 1963), pp. 176-180.

of Congress, *"it must be the policy of the United States to support free peoples who are resisting attempted subjugation by armed minorities or outside pressures." Subsequently known as the Truman Doctrine, the message was an historic departure in American foreign policy. Henceforth, the United States in peacetime would be involved militarily and economically around the world to maintain or redress the balance of power.*

Mr. President, Mr. Speaker, Members of the Congress of the United States:

THE GRAVITY OF the situation which confronts the world today necessitates my appearance before a joint session of the Congress.

The foreign policy and the national security of this country are involved.

One aspect of the present situation, which I present to you at this time for your consideration and decision, concerns Greece and Turkey.

The United States has received from the Greek Government an urgent appeal for financial and economic assistance. Preliminary reports from the American Economic Mission now in Greece and reports from the American Ambassador in Greece corroborate the statement of the Greek Government that assistance is imperative if Greece is to survive as a free nation. . . .

Greece is not a rich country. Lack of sufficient natural resources has always forced the Greek people to work hard to make both ends meet. Since 1940, this industrious, peace loving country has suffered invasion, four years of cruel enemy occupation, and bitter internal strife.

When forces of liberation entered Greece they found that the retreating Germans had destroyed virtually all the railways, roads, port facilities, communications, and merchant marine. More than a thousand villages had been burned. Eighty-five percent of the children were tubercular. Livestock, poultry, and draft animals had almost disappeared. Inflation had wiped out practically all savings.

As a result of these tragic conditions, a militant minority, exploiting human want and misery, was able to create political chaos which, until now, has made economic recovery impossible.

Greece is today without funds to finance the importation of those goods which are essential to bare subsistence. . . . Greece is in desperate need of financial and economic assistance to enable it to resume purchases of food, clothing, fuel and seeds. These are indispensable for the subsistence of its people and are obtainable only from abroad. . . .

The Greek Government has also asked for the assistance of experienced American administrators, economists and technicians to insure that the financial and other aid given to Greece shall be used effectively in creating a stable and self-sustaining economy and in improving its public administration.

The very existence of the Greek state is today threatened by the terrorist activities of several thousand armed men, led by Communists, who defy the government's authority at a number of points, particularly along the northern boundaries. . . .

Meanwhile, the Greek Government is unable to cope with the situation. The Greek army is small and poorly equipped. It needs supplies and equipment if it is to restore authority to the government throughout Greek territory. . . .

The United States must supply this assistance. . . .

No other nation is willing and able to provide the necessary support for a democratic Greek government.

The British Government, which has been helping Greece, can give no further financial or economic aid after March 31. . . .

We have considered how the United Nations might assist in this crisis. But the situation is an urgent one requiring immediate action, and the United Nations and its related organizations are not in a position to extend help of the kind that is required. . . .

The government of Greece is not perfect. Nevertheless it represents 85 percent of the members of the Greek Parliament who were chosen in an election last year. Foreign observers, including 692 Americans, considered this election to be a fair expression of the views of the Greek people. . . .

Greece's neighbor, Turkey, also deserves our attention.

The future of Turkey as an independent and economically sound state is clearly no less important to the freedom-loving peoples of the world than the future of Greece. . . .

Since the war Turkey has sought additional financial assistance from Great Britain and the United States for the purpose of effecting that modernization necessary for the maintenance of its national integrity.

That integrity is essential to the preservation of order in the Middle East.

The British Government has informed us that, owing to its own difficulties, it can no longer extend financial or economic aid to Turkey.

As in the case of Greece, if Turkey is to have the assistance it needs, the United States must supply it. We are the only country able to provide that help.

I am fully aware of the broad implications involved if the United States extends assistance to Greece and Turkey, and I shall discuss these implications with you at this time.

One of the primary objectives of the foreign policy of the United States is the creation of conditions in which we and other nations will be able to work out a way of life free from coercion. This was a fundamental issue in the war with Germany and Japan. Our victory was won over countries which sought to impose their will, and their way of life, upon other nations.

To ensure the peaceful development of nations, free from coercion, the United States has taken a leading part in establishing the United Nations. The United Nations is designed to make possible lasting freedom and independence for all its members. We shall not realize our objectives, however, unless we are willing to help free peoples to maintain their free institutions and their national integrity against aggressive movements that seek to impose upon them totalitarian regimes. This is no more than a frank recognition that totalitarian regimes imposed upon free peoples, by direct or indirect aggression, undermine the foundations of international peace and hence the security of the United States. . . .

I believe that it must be the policy of the United States to support free peoples who are resisting attempted subjugation by armed minorities or by outside pressures.

I believe that we must assist free peoples to work out their own destinies in their own way.

I believe that our help should be primarily through economic and financial aid which is essential to economic stability and orderly political processes. . . .

It is necessary only to glance at a map to realize that the survival and integrity of the Greek nation are of grave importance in a much wider situation. If Greece should fall under the control of an armed minority, the effect upon its neighbor, Turkey, would be immediate and serious. Confusion and disorder might well spread throughout the entire Middle East.

Moreover, the disappearance of Greece as an independent state would have a profound effect upon those countries in Europe whose peoples are struggling against great difficulties to maintain their freedoms and their independence while they repair the damages of war.

It would be an unspeakable tragedy if these countries, which have struggled so long against overwhelming odds, should lose that victory for which they sacrificed so much. Collapse of free institutions and loss of independence would be disastrous not only for them but for the world. . . .

We must take immediate and resolute action.

I therefore ask the Congress to provide authority for assistance to Greece and Turkey in the amount of $400,000,000 for the period ending June 30, 1948. . . .

In addition to funds, I ask the Congress to authorize the detail of American civilian and military personnel to Greece and Turkey, at the request of those countries, to assist in the tasks of reconstruction, and for the purpose of supervising the use of such financial and material assistance as may be furnished. I recommend that authority also be provided for the instruction and training of selected Greek and Turkish personnel.

Finally, I ask that the Congress provide authority which will permit the speediest and most effective use, in terms of needed commodities, supplies, and equipment, of such funds as may be authorized.

If further funds, or further authority, should be needed for the purposes indicated in this message, I shall not hesitate to bring the situation before the Congress. On this subject the Executive and Legislative branches of the Government must work together.

This is a serious course upon which we embark.

I would not recommend it except that the alternative is much more serious.

The United States contributed $341,000,000,000 toward winning World War II. This is an investment in world freedom and world peace.

The assistance that I am recommending for Greece and Turkey amounts to little more than $\frac{1}{10}$ of 1 percent of this investment. It is only common sense that we should safeguard this investment and make sure that it was not in vain.

The seeds of totalitarian regimes are nurtured by misery and want. They spread and grow in the evil soil of poverty and strife. They reach their full growth when the hope of a people for a better life has died.

We must keep that hope alive.

The free peoples of the world look to us for support in maintaining their freedoms.

If we falter in our leadership, we may endanger the peace of the world—and we shall surely endanger the welfare of this Nation.

Great responsibilities have been placed upon us by the swift movement of events.

I am confident that the Congress will face these responsibilities squarely.

John F. Kennedy's Inaugural Address

The inaugural address by John F. Kennedy on January 20, 1961, was a ringing affirmation of America's global responsibilities. For the first time, a Chief Executive in taking the oath of office devoted his entire peroration in articulating his commitment and that of his nation to the proposition that "no man is an isle intyre of itself . . ."

Vice President Johnson, Mr. Speaker, Mr. Chief Justice, President Eisenhower, Vice President Nixon, President Truman, Reverend Clergy, fellow citizens:

WE OBSERVE TODAY not a victory of party but a celebration of freedom—symbolizing an end as well as a beginning—signifying renewal as well as change. For I have sworn before you and Almighty God the same solemn oath our forebears prescribed nearly a century and three quarters ago.

The world is very different now. For man holds in his mortal hands the power to abolish all forms of human poverty and all forms of human life. And yet the same revolutionary beliefs for which our forebears fought are still at issue around the globe—the belief that the rights of man come not from the generosity of the state but from the hand of God.

We dare not forget today that we are the heirs of that first revolution. Let the word go forth from this time and place, to friend and foe alike, that the torch has been passed to a new generation of Americans —born in this century, tempered by war, disciplined by a hard and bitter peace, proud of our ancient heritage—and unwilling to witness or permit the slow undoing of those human rights to which this nation has always been committed, and to which we are committed today at home and around the world.

Let every nation know, whether it wishes us well or ill, that we shall pay any price, bear any burden, meet any hardship, support any friend, oppose any foe to assure the survival and the success of liberty.

Public Papers of the Presidents of the United States, John F. Kennedy, 1961 *(Washington, D.C.: U.S. Government Printing Office, 1962), pp. 1-3.*

This much we pledge—and more.

To those old allies whose cultural and spiritual origins we share, we pledge the loyalty of faithful friends. United, there is little we cannot do in a host of cooperative ventures. Divided, there is little we can do—for we dare not meet a powerful challenge at odds and split asunder.

To those new states whom we welcome to the ranks of the free, we pledge our word that one form of colonial control shall not have passed away merely to be replaced by a far more iron tyranny. We shall not always expect to find them supporting our view. But we shall always hope to find them strongly supporting their own freedom—and to remember that, in the past, those who foolishly sought power by riding the back of the tiger ended up inside.

To those peoples in the huts and villages of half the globe struggling to break the bonds of mass misery, we pledge our best efforts to help them help themselves, for whatever period is required—not because the communists may be doing it, not because we seek their votes, but because it is right. If a free society cannot help the many who are poor, it cannot save the few who are rich.

To our sister republics south of our border, we offer a special pledge —to convert our good words into good deeds—in a new alliance for progress—to assist free men and free governments in casting off the chains of poverty. But this peaceful revolution of hope cannot become the prey of hostile powers. Let all our neighbors know that we shall join with them to oppose aggression or subversion anywhere in the Americas. And let every other power know that this Hemisphere intends to remain the master of its own house.

To that world assembly of sovereign states, the United Nations, our last best hope in an age where the instruments of war have far outpaced the instruments of peace, we renew our pledge of support—to prevent it from becoming merely a forum for invective—to strengthen its shield of the new and the weak—and to enlarge the area in which its writ may run.

Finally, to those nations who would make themselves our adversary, we offer not a pledge but a request: that both sides begin anew the quest for peace, before the dark powers of destruction unleashed by science engulf all humanity in planned or accidental self-destruction.

We dare not tempt them with weakness. For only when our arms are sufficient beyond doubt can we be certain beyond doubt that they will never be employed.

But neither can two great and powerful groups of nations take comfort from our present course—both sides overburdened by the cost of modern weapons, both rightly alarmed by the steady spread of the deadly atom, yet both racing to alter that uncertain balance of terror that stays the hand of mankind's final war.

So let us begin anew—remembering on both sides that civility is not a sign of weakness, and sincerity is always subject to proof. Let us never negotiate out of fear. But let us never fear to negotiate.

Let both sides explore what problems unite us instead of belaboring those problems which divide us.

Let both sides, for the first time, formulate serious and precise proposals for the inspection and control of arms—and bring the absolute power to destroy other nations under the absolute control of all nations.

Let both sides seek to invoke the wonders of science instead of its terrors. Together let us explore the stars, conquer the deserts, eradicate disease, tap the ocean depths and encourage the arts and commerce.

Let both sides unite to heed in all corners of the earth the command of Isaiah—to "undo the heavy burdens . . . (and) let the oppressed go free."

And if a beach-head of cooperation may push back the jungle of suspicion, let both sides join in creating a new endeavor, not a new balance of power, but a new world of law, where the strong are just and the weak secure and the peace preserved.

All this will not be finished in the first one hundred days. Nor will it be finished in the first one thousand days, nor in the life of this Administration, nor even perhaps in our lifetime on this planet. But let us begin.

In your hands, my fellow citizens, more than mine, will rest the final success or failure of our course. Since this country was founded, each generation of Americans has been summoned to give testimony to its national loyalty. The graves of young Americans who answered the call to service surround the globe.

Now the trumpet summons us again—not as a call to bear arms, though arms we need—not as a call to battle, though embattled we are —but a call to bear the burden of a long twilight struggle, year in and year out, "rejoicing in hope, patient in tribulation"—a struggle against the common enemies of man: tyranny, poverty, disease and war itself.

Can we forge against these enemies a grand and global alliance, North and South, East and West, that can assure a more fruitful life for all mankind? Will you join in that historic effort?

In the long history of the world, only a few generations have been granted the role of defending freedom in its hour of maximum danger. I do not shrink from this responsibility—I welcome it. I do not believe that any of us would exchange places with any other people or any other generation. The energy, the faith, the devotion which we bring to this endeavor will light our country and all who serve it—and the glow from that fire can truly light the world.

And so, my fellow Americans: ask not what your country can do for you—ask what you can do for your country.

My fellow citizens of the world: ask not what America will do for you, but what together we can do for the freedom of man.

Finally, whether you are citizens of America or citizens of the world, ask of us here the same high standards of strength and sacrifice which we ask of you. With a good conscience our only sure reward, with history the final judge of our deeds, let us go forth to lead the land we love, asking His blessing and His help, but knowing that here on earth God's work must truly be our own.

5

Director of the Economy

The pivotal role of the twentieth-century President in the nation's economic affairs has put his office at another vital center of power. With government an active participant in the economy, the President has become the director of its overall destiny. A measure of the continuing trend in this area—from the Square Deal of Theodore Roosevelt to the New Freedom of Woodrow Wilson to the New Deal of Franklin D. Roosevelt—is the institutionalization of this presidential function by the Employment Act of 1946.

For an assessment of the nation's economic "health," the President relies upon the expertise of his Council of Economic Advisors. Economic indicators, such as the international balance of payments, the gross national product, the level of employment, and the consumer price indices, all come within his purview and are his direct concern. In reporting annually to Congress on the nation's economy, the President is required, whenever necessary, to recommend measures that would contribute to its well being. If an economic recession or depression threatens, he is expected to take action—either by invoking his executive authority or by urging Congress to enact emergency measures. This dimension of presidential leadership, a concomitant of contemporary society, could not have been imagined by earlier Presidents who operated in a laissez-faire *climate.*

The Employment Act of 1946

AN ACT

TO DECLARE A national policy on employment, production, and purchasing power, and for other purposes.

Be it enacted by the Senate and House of Representatives of the United States of America in Congress assembled,

SHORT TITLE

SECTION 1. This Act may be cited as the "Employment Act of 1946."

DECLARATION OF POLICY

SEC. 2. The Congress hereby declares that it is the continuing policy and responsibility of the Federal Government to use all practicable means consistent with its needs and obligations and other essential considerations of national policy, with the assistance and cooperation of industry, agriculture, labor, and State and local governments, to coordinate and utilize all its plans, functions, and resources for the purpose of creating and maintaining, in a manner calculated to foster and promote free competitive enterprise and the general welfare, conditions under which there will be afforded useful employment opportunities, including self-employment, for those able, willing, and seeking to work, and to promote maximum employment, production, and purchasing power.

ECONOMIC REPORT OF THE PRESIDENT

SEC. 3. (a) The President shall transmit to the Congress within sixty days after the beginning of each regular session (commencing with the year 1947) an economic report (hereinafter called the "Economic

Congressional Record, *79th Congress, 2nd Session (February 20, 1946), pp. 23-26.*

Report") setting forth (1) the levels of employment, production, and purchasing power obtaining in the United States and such levels needed to carry out the policy declared in section 2; (2) current and foreseeable trends in the levels of employment, production, and purchasing power; (3) a review of the economic program of the Federal Government and a review of economic conditions affecting employment in the United States or any considerable portion thereof during the preceding year and of their effect upon employment, production, and purchasing power; and (4) a program for carrying out the policy declared in section 2, together with such recommendations for legislation as he may deem necessary or desirable.

(b) The President may transmit from time to time to the Congress reports supplementary to the Economic Report, each of which shall include such supplementary or revised recommendations as he may deem necessary or desirable to achieve the policy declared in section 2.

(c) The Economic Report, and all supplementary reports transmitted under subsection (b), shall, when transmitted to Congress, be referred to the joint committee created by section 5.

COUNCIL OF ECONOMIC ADVISERS TO THE PRESIDENT

SEC. 4. (a) There is hereby created in the Executive Office of the President a Council of Economic Advisers (hereinafter called the "Council"). The Council shall be composed of three members who shall be appointed by the President, by and with the advice and consent of the Senate, and each of whom shall be a person who, as a result of his training, experience, and attainments, is exceptionally qualified to analyze and interpret economic developments, to appraise programs and activities of the Government in the light of the policy declared in section 2, and to formulate and recommend national economic policy to promote employment, production, and purchasing power under free competitive enterprise. Each member of the Council shall receive compensation at the rate of $15,000 per annum. The President shall designate one of the members of the Council as chairman and one as vice chairman, who shall act as chairman in the absence of the chairman.

(b) The Council is authorized to employ, and fix the compensation of, such specialists and other experts as may be necessary for the carrying out of its functions under this Act, without regard to the civil-service laws and the Classification Act of 1923, as amended, and is authorized, subject to the civil-service laws, to employ such other officers and employees as may be necessary for carrying out its functions under this

Act, and fix their compensation in accordance with the Classification Act of 1923, as amended.

(c) It shall be the duty and function of the Council—

(1) to assist and advise the President in the preparation of the Economic Report;

(2) to gather timely and authoritative information concerning economic developments and economic trends, both current and prospective, to analyze and interpret such information in the light of the policy declared in section 2 for the purpose of determining whether such developments and trends are interfering, or are likely to interfere, with the achievement of such policy, and to compile and submit to the President studies relating to such developments and trends;

(3) to appraise the various programs and activities of the Federal Government in the light of the policy declared in section 2 for the purpose of determining the extent to which such programs and activities are contributing, and the extent to which they are not contributing, to the achievement of such policy, and to make recommendations to the President with respect thereto;

(4) to develop and recommend to the President national economic policies to foster and promote free competitive enterprise, to avoid economic fluctuations or to diminish the effects thereof, and to maintain employment, production, and purchasing power;

(5) to make and furnish such studies, reports thereon, and recommendations with respect to matters of Federal economic policy and legislation as the President may request.

(d) The Council shall make an annual report to the President in December of each year.

(e) In exercising its powers, functions and duties under this Act—

(1) the Council may constitute such advisory committees and may consult with such representatives of industry, agriculture, labor, consumers, State and local governments, and other groups, as it deems advisable;

(2) the Council shall, to the fullest extent possible, utilize the services, facilities, and information (including statistical information) of other Government agencies as well as of private research agencies, in order that duplication of effort and expense may be avoided.

(f) To enable the Council to exercise its powers, functions, and duties under this Act, there are authorized to be appropriated (except for the salaries of the members and the salaries of officers and employees of the Council) such sums as may be necessary. For the salaries of the members and the salaries of officers and employees of the Council, there is authorized to be appropriated not exceeding $345,000 in the aggregate for each fiscal year. . . .

6

The President and Social Justice

The transformation of the United States from a predominantly rural into an industrial society with laboring masses, congested cities, slums, choked highways, and underprivileged minorities demanded a new response from government. Increasingly, it was the President, the only official elected by all the people, who has assumed responsibility for the general welfare. The major social and economic reforms of this century have been initiated by the Chief Executive. Special interests have their champions in Congress, but the people at large look to the White House.

Given the contemporary configurations of the Electoral College, with its large blocs of rates in the urban and industrial states, the modern President can be depended upon to press for governmental measures designed to widen opportunities for all and to ameliorate some of the nation's grievous social ills. This twentieth-century aspect of leadership is another factor in the growth of the power and the prestige of the Presidency.

President's Committee on Civil Rights

EXECUTIVE ORDER 9808

ESTABLISHING THE PRESIDENT'S COMMITTEE ON CIVIL RIGHTS

WHEREAS THE PRESERVATION of civil rights guaranteed by the Constitution is essential to domestic tranquility, national security, the general welfare, and the continued existence of our free institutions; and

Federal Register, *11, No. 244 (December 7, 1946), 14153.*

Whereas the action of individuals who take the law into their own hands and inflict summary punishment and wreak personal vengeance is subversive of our democratic system of law enforcement and public criminal justice, and gravely threatens our form of government; and

Whereas it is essential that all possible steps be taken to safeguard our civil rights:

Now, therefore, by virtue of the authority vested in me as President of the United States by the Constitution and the statutes of the United States, it is hereby ordered as follows:

1. There is hereby created a committee to be known as the President's Committee on Civil Rights, which shall be composed of the following-named members, who shall serve without compensation: . . .

2. The Committee is authorized on behalf of the President to inquire into and to determine whether and in what respect current law-enforcement measures and the authority and means possessed by Federal, State, and local governments may be strengthened and improved to safeguard the civil rights of the people.

3. All executive departments and agencies of the Federal Government are authorized and directed to cooperate with the Committee in its work, and to furnish the Committee such information or the services of such persons as the Committee may require in the performance of its duties.

4. When requested by the Committee to do so, persons employed in any of the executive departments and agencies of the Federal Government shall testify before the Committee and shall make available for the use of the Committee such documents and other information as the Committee may require.

5. The Committee shall make a report of its studies to the President in writing, and shall in particular make recommendations with respect to the adoption or establishment, by legislation or otherwise, of more adequate and effective means and procedures for the protection of the civil rights of the people of the United States.

6. Upon rendition of its report to the President, the Committee shall cease to exist, unless otherwise determined by further Executive order.

HARRY S TRUMAN

THE WHITE HOUSE,
December 5, 1946.

President Johnson's Proposal for Massive Federal Aid to Education (*Jan. 12, 1965*)

TO THE CONGRESS OF THE UNITED STATES:

IN 1787, the Continental Congress declared in the Northwest Ordinance: "schools and the means of education shall forever be encouraged."

America is strong and prosperous and free because for one hundred and seventy-eight years we have honored that commitment.

In the United States today:

One-quarter of all Americans are in the nation's classrooms.

High school attendance has grown 18-fold since the turn of the century—6 times as fast as the population.

College enrollment has advanced 80-fold. Americans today support a fourth of the world's institutions of higher learning and a third of its professors and college students.

In the life of the individual, education is always an unfinished task.

And in the life of this nation, the advancement of education is a continuing challenge.

There is a darker side to education in America:

One student out of every three now in the fifth grade will drop out before finishing high school—if the present rate continues.

Almost a million young people will continue to quit school each year—if our schools fail to stimulate their desire to learn.

Over one hundred thousand of our brightest high school graduates each year will not go to college—and many others will leave college—if the opportunity for higher education is not expanded.

The cost of this neglect runs high—both for the youth and the nation.

Unemployment of young people with an eighth grade education or less is four times the national average.

Jobs filled by high school graduates rose by 40 percent in the last ten years. Jobs for those with less schooling decreased by nearly 10 percent.

We can measure the cost in even starker terms. We now spend about $450 a year per child in our public schools. But we spend $1800 a year to keep a delinquent youth in a detention home, $2500 a year for a family on relief, $3500 a year for a criminal in state prison.

The growing numbers of young people reaching school age demand that we move swiftly even to stand still.

Attendance in elementary and secondary schools will increase by 4 million in the next five years. 400,000 new classrooms will be needed to meet this growth. But over 1½ million of the nation's existing classrooms are already more than 30 years old.

The post-World War II boom in babies has now reached college age. And by 1970, our colleges must be prepared to add 50 per cent more enrollment to their presently overcrowded facilities.

In the past, Congress has supported an increasing commitment to education in America. Last year, I signed historic measures passed by the Eighty-eighth Congress to provide:

facilities badly needed by universities, colleges and community colleges;

major new resources for vocational training;

more loans and fellowships for students enrolled in higher education;

enlarged and improved training for physicians, dentists and nurses.

I propose that the Eighty-ninth Congress join me in extending the commitment still further. I propose that we declare a national goal of *Full Educational Opportunity*.

Every child must be encouraged to get as much education as he has the ability to take.

We want this not only for his sake—but for the nation's sake.

Nothing matters more to the future of our country: not our military preparedness—for armed might is worthless if we lack the brain power to build a world of peace; not our productive economy—for we cannot sustain growth without trained manpower; not our democratic system of government—for freedom is fragile if citizens are ignorant.

We must demand that our schools increase not only the quantity but the quality of America's education. For we recognize that nuclear age problems cannot be solved with horse-and-buggy learning. The three *R's* of our school system must be supported by the three *T's*—*teachers* who are superior, *techniques* of instruction that are modern, and *thinking* about education which places it first in all our plans and hopes.

Specifically, four major tasks confront us:

to bring better education to millions of disadvantaged youth who need it most;

to put the best educational equipment and ideas and innovations within reach of all students;

to advance the technology of teaching and the training of teachers;

to provide incentives for those who wish to learn at every stage along the road to learning.

Our program must match the magnitude of these tasks. The budget on education which I request for fiscal year 1966 will contain a total of $4.1 billion. This includes $1.1 billion to finance programs established by the Eighty-eighth Congress. I will submit a request for $1.5 billion in new obligational authority to finance the programs described in this message. This expenditure is a small price to pay for developing our nation's most priceless resource.

In all that we do, we mean to strengthen our state and community education systems. Federal assistance does not mean federal control—as past programs have proven. The late Senator Robert Taft declared: "Education is primarily a state function—but in the field of education, as in the fields of health, relief and medical care, the Federal Government has a secondary obligation to see that there is a basic floor under those essential services for all adults and children in the United States."

In this spirit, I urge that we now push ahead with the number one business of the American people—the education of our youth in pre-schools, elementary and secondary schools, and in the colleges and universities. . . .

7

Party Leader

American political parties are basically loose coalitions of disparate elements. Lacking any ideological cohesion or formal membership, their primary purpose is to win office. Congressmen, accordingly, are free to support or reject legislative recommendations adopted by their own party's national convention. In the absence of any structural provision for party responsibility, it is the President who is expected to lead the party and help it to achieve unity of purpose.

This particular presidential role was not anticipated by the framers of the Constitution, because they did not foresee the rise of political parties. After the emergence of parties, those Presidents who sought to make the most effective use of their leadership found them invaluable tools.

Elected by a nationwide constituency, the President can draw upon his power and popularity to mobilize the party in support of his legislative program. He can employ patronage as an instrument of coercion or persuasion, use the great prestige of his office to support candidates seeking election to Congress, and employ party gatherings to galvanize sentiment in favor of his programs. Yet a President must tread warily, lest his meddling in intra-party feuds backfires. Franklin D. Roosevelt discovered this danger when, in his attempt to influence the selection of candidates friendly to his New Deal program, he interfered in party primaries.

Yet the modern President must be first and foremost a politician and a willing combatant in the political arena. He cannot remain above the political battle if he hopes to achieve his purposes and to leave behind him a legacy of noteworthy accomplishment.

Incensed by the constant efforts of conservative Democrats in Congress to thwart his New Deal program, President Roosevelt sought to have a number of them retired to private life. In the 1938 elections he endeavored to bring about their defeat by campaigning against them during their primary contests while supporting candidates loyal to his legislative program. Below is an address which Roosevelt gave in pursuit of this objective.

Franklin D. Roosevelt at Barnesville, Georgia, August 10, 1938

. . . THAT IS WHY the longer I live, the more am I convinced that there are two types of political leadership which are dangerous to the continuation of broad economic and social progress all along that long battlefront. The first type of political leadership which is dangerous to progress is represented by the man who harps on one or two remedies or proposals and claims that these one or two remedies will cure all our

Samuel I. Rosenman, ed., Public Papers and Addresses of Franklin D. Roosevelt, 1938 (N.Y., Macmillan Co., 1941), pp. 465-470. Copyright, 1941, Estate of Franklin D. Roosevelt. Reprinted by permission of the Estate of Franklin D. Roosevelt and Samuel I. Rosenman.

ills. The other type of dangerous leadership is represented by the man who says that he is in favor of progress but whose record shows that he hinders or hampers or tries to kill new measures of progress. He is that type of political leader who tells his friends that he does not like this or that or the other detail; and, at the same time, he utterly fails to offer a substitute that is practical or worthwhile.

The task of meeting the economic and social needs of the South, on the broad front that is absolutely necessary, calls for public servants whose hearts are sound, whose heads are sane—whose hands are strong, striving everlastingly to better the lot of their fellowmen.

The report to which I referred is a synopsis—a clear listing of the economic and social problems of the Southland. It suggests the many steps that must be taken to solve the problems.

Some of these steps, it is true, can be taken by state governments, but you will readily realize that action by the states alone, even if such action on the part of many neighboring states could be simultaneous and immediate, would be wholly inadequate. The very good reason for that is that most of these problems involve interstate relationships, relationships not only among the states of this region but also between each and all of these states and the rest of the Nation.

It is not an attack on state sovereignty to point out that this national aspects of all these problems requires action by the Federal Government in Washington. I do not hesitate to say from long experience that during the past five years there has been a closer and more effective peacetime cooperation between the Governors of the forty-eight states and the President of the United States than at any other time in our whole national history.

You are familiar enough with the processes of Government to know that the Chief Executive cannot take action on national or regional problems, unless they have been first translated into Acts of Congress passed by the Senate and the House of Representatives of the United States.

Such action by the Congress, it is equally clear, must be vigorously supported by the Senators and Representatives whose constituents are directly concerned with Southern economics and Southern social needs. Senators and Congressmen who are not wholeheartedly in sympathy with these needs cannot be expected to give them vigorous support.

Translating that into more intimate terms, it means that if the people of the State of Georgia want definite action in the Congress of the United States, they must send to that Congress Senators and Representatives who are willing to stand up and fight night and day for Federal statutes drawn to meet actual needs—not something that serves merely to gloss over the evils of the moment for the time being—but laws with teeth in them which go to the root of the problems; which remove the inequities, raise the standards and, over a period of years, give constant improvement to the conditions of human life in this State.

You, the people of Georgia, in the coming Senatorial primary, for example, have a perfect right to choose any candidate you wish. I do not seek to impair that right, and I am not going to impair that right of the people of this State; but because Georgia has been good enough to call me her adopted son and because for many long years I have regarded Georgia as my "other state," I feel no hesitation in telling you what I would do if I could vote here next month. I am strengthened in that decision to give you my personal opinion of the coming Senatorial primary by the fact that during the past few weeks I have had many requests from distinguished citizens of Georgia—from people high and low— from the Chief Justice of the highest court of Georgia and many others.

Let me preface my statement by saying that I have personally known three of the candidates for the United States Senate for many years. All of them have had legislative or executive experience as Government servants. We may therefore justly consider their records and their public utterances—and we can justly, also, seek to determine for ourselves what is their inward point of view in relationship to present and future problems of government.

It has been pointed out by writers and speakers who do not analyze public questions very deeply that in passing through the State of Kentucky a month ago I gave as a reason for the reelection of Senator Barkley that he had had very long and successful service in the Congress of the United States and that his opponent did not have that experience. In Kentucky, there was no clear-cut issue between a liberal on the one side and a dyed-in-the-wool conservative on the other. Neither of the two principals on his record could be classified as a reactionary; therefore, the criterion of experience, especially that of the Majority Leadership of the Senate of the United States, weighed heavily, and properly, in favor of Senator Barkley.

Here in Georgia, however, my old friend, the senior Senator from this State, cannot possibly in my judgment be classified as belonging to the liberal school of thought—and, therefore, the argument that he has long served in the Senate falls by the wayside. Here in Georgia the issue is a different one from that in Kentucky.

I speak seriously and in the most friendly way in terms of liberal and conservative for the very simple fact that on my shoulders rests a responsibility to the people of the United States. In 1932 and again in 1936 I was chosen Chief Executive with the mandate to seek by definite action to correct many evils of the past and of the present; to work for a wider distribution of national income, to improve the conditions of life, especially among those who need it most and, above all, to use every honest effort to keep America in the van of social and economic progress.

To the Congress of the United States I make recommendations— that is all—in most cases recommendations relating to objectives, leaving it to the Congress to translate the recommendations into law. The majority of the Senate and House have agreed with those objectives, and have worked with me; and I have worked with them to translate those objectives into action. Some have given "lip service" to some of the objectives but have not raised their little fingers actively to attain the objectives themselves. Too often these few have listened to the dictatorship of a small minority of individuals and corporations who oppose the objectives themselves. That is a real dictatorship and one which we have been getting away from slowly but surely during the past five years. As long as I live, you will find me fighting against any kind of dictatorship —especially the kind of dictatorship which has enslaved many of our fellow citizens for more than half a century.

What I am about to say will be no news, to my old friend—and I say it with the utmost sincerity—Senator Walter George. It will be no surprise to him because I have recently had personal correspondence with him; and, as a result of it, he fully knows what my views are.

Let me make it clear that he is, and I hope always will be, my personal friend. He is beyond question, beyond any possible question, a gentleman and a scholar; but there are other gentlemen in the Senate and in the House for whom I have a real affectionate regard, but with whom I differ heartily and sincerely on the principles and policies of how the Government of the United States ought to be run.

For example, I have had an almost lifelong acquaintance and great personal friendship for people like Senator Hale from the State of Maine, for Representative James Wadsworth of New York and for the Minority Leader, Representative Snell. All of these lifelong conservative Republicans are gentlemen and scholars; but they and I learned long ago that our views on public questions were just as wide apart as the North Pole and the South.

Therefore, I repeat that I trust, and am confident, that Senator George and I shall always be good personal friends even though I am impelled to make it clear that on most public questions he and I do not speak the same language.

To carry out my responsibility as President, it is clear that if there is to be success in our Government there ought to be cooperation between members of my own party and myself—cooperation, in other words, within the majority party, between one branch of Government, the Legislative branch, and the head of the other branch, the Executive. That is one of the essentials of a party form of government. It has been going on in this country for nearly a century and a half. The test is not measured, in the case of an individual, by his every vote on every bill —of course not. The test lies rather in the answer to two questions: first, has the record of the candidate shown, while differing perhaps in details, a constant active fighting attitude in favor of the broad objectives of the party and of the Government as they are constituted today; and, secondly, does the candidate really, in his heart, deep down in his heart, believe in those objectives? I regret that in the case of my friend, Senator George, I cannot honestly answer either of these questions in the affirmative.

In the case of another candidate in the State of Georgia for the United States Senate—former Governor Talmadge—I have known him for many years. His attitude toward me and toward other members of the Government in 1935 and in 1936 concerns me not at all. But, in those years and in this year I have read so many of his proposals, so many of his promises, so many of his panaceas, that I am very certain in my own mind that his election would contribute very little to practical progress in government. That is all I can say about him.

The third candidate that I would speak of, United States Attorney Lawrence Camp, I have also known for many years. He has had experience in the State Legislature; he has served as Attorney General of Georgia for four years; he has made a distinguished record in the United States District Court, his office ranking among the first two in the whole of the United States in the expedition of Federal cases in that Court. I regard him not only as a public servant with successful experience but as a man who honestly believes that many things must be done and done now to improve the economic and social conditions of the country, a man who is willing to fight for these objectives. Fighting ability is of the utmost importance.

Therefore, answering the requests that have come to me from many leading citizens of Georgia that I make my position clear, I have no hesitation in saying that if I were able to vote in the September primaries in this State, I most assuredly should cast my ballot for Lawrence Camp.

8

The President and Public Opinion

No one in the country has such ready access to the public ear as does the President. If he expresses his views at a press conference, delivers a "fireside chat," speaks on some ceremonial occasion or political rally, or makes informal remarks to a visiting statesman, he commands the attention of the entire world. Yet, at a time when the most sophisticated mechanisms of instant, mass communication are available to him, the complex nature of the national and international situation often frustrates his effort to influence public opinion in the manner required by the national interest. Strategically situated to be the nation's chief educator, he frequently finds it difficult, if not impossible, to dispel myths which have become entrenched in public mind.

A perennial problem, which each President must solve for himself, is when to lead and when to follow. When must prudence dictate his choice, or when should he be bold instead of cautious? Does he have a moral right to practice deception when he believes that the nation's security is at stake?

One vital aspect of leadership in public opinion is style. The character of the administration will set the tone for the entire country. With drift in the White House, the nation will drift; with complacency, the nation will lapse into apathy. On the other hand, if the President demonstrates a regard for excellence, if he sets meaningful goals and exhibits a sense of expectancy and dedication of purpose, he will spark a dynamic response from the people.

The following selection, a commencement address by President Kennedy, delivered at American University, in Washington, D.C., 1963, deals with fundamental questions of foreign policy. Subjecting some widely held myths to critical scrutiny, President Kennedy sought to show that continued adherence to these beliefs militates against an enlightened approach and thereby retards progress.

John F. Kennedy—The American University Address, June 10, 1963

President Anderson, members of the faculty, board of trustees, distinguished guests, my old colleague, Senator Bob Byrd, who has earned his degree through many years of attending night law school, while I am earning mine in the next 30 minutes, ladies and gentlemen:

IT IS WITH great pride that I participate in this ceremony of the American University, sponsored by the Methodist Church, founded by Bishop John Fletcher Hurst, and first opened by President Woodrow Wilson in 1914. This is a young and growing university, but it has already fulfilled Bishop Hurst's enlightened hope for the study of history and public affairs in a city devoted to the making of history and to the conduct of the public's business. By sponsoring this institution of higher learning for all who wish to learn, whatever their color or their creed, the Methodists of this area and the Nation deserve the Nation's thanks, and I commend all those who are today graduating.

Professor Woodrow Wilson once said that every man sent out from a university should be a man of his nation as well as a man of his time, and I am confident that the men and women who carry the honor of graduating from this institution will continue to give from their lives, from their talents, a high measure of public service and public support.

"There are few earthly things more beautiful than a university," wrote John Masefield, in his tribute to English universities—and his words are equally true today. He did not refer to spires and towers, to campus greens and ivied walls. He admired the splendid beauty of the university, he said, because it was "a place where those who hate ignorance may strive to know, where those who perceive truth may strive to make others see."

I have, therefore, chosen this time and this place to discuss a topic on which ignorance too often abounds and the truth is too rarely perceived—yet it is the most important topic on earth: world peace.

What kind of peace do I mean? What kind of peace do we seek? Not a Pax Americana enforced on the world by American weapons of war.

Public Papers of the Presidents of the United States, John F. Kennedy, 1963 (Washington, D.C.: U.S. Government Printing Office, 1964), pp. 459-464.

Not the peace of the grave or the security of the slave. I am talking about genuine peace, the kind of peace that makes life on earth worth living, the kind that enables men and nations to grow and to hope and to build a better life for their children—not merely peace for Americans but peace for all men and women—not merely peace in our time but peace for all time.

I speak of peace because of the new face of war. Total war makes no sense in an age when great powers can maintain large and relatively invulnerable nuclear forces and refuse to surrender without resort to those forces. It makes no sense in an age when a single nuclear weapon contains almost ten times the explosive force delivered by all of the allied air forces in the Second World War. It makes no sense in an age when the deadly poisons produced by a nuclear exchange would be carried by wind and water and soil and seed to the far corners of the globe and to generations yet unborn.

Today the expenditure of billions of dollars every year on weapons acquired for the purpose of making sure we never need to use them is essential to keeping the peace. But surely the acquisition of such idle stockpiles—which can only destroy and never create—is not the only, much less the most efficient, means of assuring peace.

I speak of peace, therefore, as the necessary rational end of rational men. I realize that the pursuit of peace is not as dramatic as the pursuit of war—and frequently the words of the pursuer fall on deaf ears. But we have no more urgent task.

Some say that it is useless to speak of world peace or world law or world disarmament—and that it will be useless until the leaders of the Soviet Union adopt a more enlightened attitude. I hope they do. I believe we can help them do it. But I also believe that we must reexamine our own attitude—as individuals and as a Nation—for our attitude is as essential as theirs. And every graduate of this school, every thoughtful citizen who despairs of war and wishes to bring peace, should begin by looking inward—by examining his own attitude toward the possibilities of peace, toward the Soviet Union, toward the course of the cold war and toward freedom and peace here at home.

First: Let us examine our attitude toward peace itself. Too many of us think it is impossible. Too many think it unreal. But that is a dangerous, defeatist belief. It leads to the conclusion that war is inevitable—that mankind is doomed—that we are gripped by forces we cannot control.

We need not accept that view. Our problems are manmade—therefore, they can be solved by man. And man can be as big as he wants. No problem of human destiny is beyond human beings. Man's reason and spirit have often solved the seemingly unsolvable—and we believe they can do it again.

I am not referring to the absolute, infinite concept of universal peace and good will of which some fantasies and fanatics dream. I do not deny the value of hopes and dreams but we merely invite discouragement and incredulity by making that our only and immediate goal.

Let us focus instead on a more practical, more attainable peace—based not on a sudden revolution in human nature but on a gradual evolution in human institutions—on a series of concrete actions and effective agreements which are in the interest of all concerned. There is no single, simple key to this peace—no grand or magic formula to be adopted by one or two powers. Genuine peace must be the product of many nations, the sum of many acts. It must be dynamic, not static, changing to meet the challenge of each new generation. For peace is a process—a way of solving problems.

With such a peace, there will still be quarrels and conflicting interests, as there are within families and nations. World peace, like community peace, does not require that each man love his neighbor—it requires only that they live together in mutual tolerance, submitting their disputes to a just and peaceful settlement. And history teaches us that enmities between nations, as between individuals, do not last forever. However fixed our likes and dislikes may seem, the tide of time and events will often bring surprising changes in the relations between nations and neighbors.

So let us persevere. Peace need not be impracticable, and war need not be inevitable. By defining our goal more clearly, by making it seem more manageable and less remote, we can help all peoples to see it, to draw hope from it, and to move irresistibly toward it.

Second: Let us reexamine our attitude toward the Soviet Union. It is discouraging to think that their leaders may actually believe what their propagandists write. It is discouraging to read a recent authoritative Soviet text on *Military Strategy* and find, on page after page, wholly baseless and incredible claims—such as the allegation that "American imperialist circles are preparing to unleash different types of wars . . . that there is a very real threat of a preventive war being unleashed by American imperialists against the Soviet Union . . . [and that] the political aims of the American imperialists are to enslave economically and politically the European and other capitalist countries . . . [and] to achieve world domination . . . by means of aggressive wars."

Truly, as it was written long ago: "The wicked flee when no man pursueth." Yet it is sad to read these Soviet statements—to realize the extent of the gulf between us. But it is also a warning—a warning to the American people not to fall into the same trap as the Soviets, not to see only a distorted and desperate view of the other side, not to see conflict as inevitable, accommodation as impossible, and communication as nothing more than an exchange of threats.

No government or social system is so evil that its people must be considered as lacking in virtue. As Americans, we find communism profoundly repugnant as a negation of personal freedom and dignity. But we can still hail the Russian people for their many achievements—in science and space, in economic and industrial growth, in culture and in acts of courage.

Among the many traits the peoples of our two countries have in common, none is stronger than our mutual abhorrence of war. Almost unique, among the major world powers, we have never been at war with each other. And no nation in the history of battle ever suffered more than the Soviet Union suffered in the course of the Second World War. At least 20 million lost their lives. Countless millions of homes and farms were burned or sacked. A third of the nation's territory, including nearly two thirds of its industrial base, was turned into a wasteland—a loss equivalent to the devastation of this country east of Chicago.

Today, should total war ever break out again—no matter how—our two countries would become the primary targets. It is an ironic but accurate fact that the two strongest powers are the two in the most danger of devastation. All we have built, all we have worked for, would be destroyed in the first 24 hours. And even in the cold war, which brings burdens and dangers to so many countries, including this Nation's closest allies—our two countries bear the heaviest burdens. For we are both devoting massive sums of money to weapons that could be better devoted to combating ignorance, poverty, and disease. We are both caught up in a vicious and dangerous cycle in which suspicion on one side breeds suspicion on the other, and new weapons beget counterweapons.

In short, both the United States and its allies, and the Soviet Union and its allies, have a mutually deep interest in a just and genuine peace and in halting the arms race. Agreements to this end are in the interest of the Soviet Union as well as ours—and even the most hostile nations can be relied upon to accept and keep those treaty obligations, and only those treaty obligations, which are in their own interest.

So, let us not be blind to our differences—but let us also direct attention to our common interests and to the means by which those differences can be resolved. And if we cannot end now our differences, at least we can help make the world safe for diversity. For, in the final analysis, our most basic common link is that we all inhabit this small planet. We all breathe the same air. We all cherish our children's future. And we are all mortal.

Third: Let us reexamine our attitude toward the cold war, remembering that we are not engaged in a debate, seeking to pile up debating points. We are not here distributing blame or pointing the finger of judgment. We must deal with the world as it is, and not as it might have been had the history of the last 18 years been different.

We must, therefore, persevere in the search for peace in the hope that constructive changes within the Communist bloc might bring within reach solutions which now seem beyond us. We must conduct our affairs in such a way that it becomes in the Communists' interest to agree on a genuine peace. Above all, while defending our own vital interests, nuclear powers must avert those confrontations which bring an adversary to a choice of either a humiliating retreat or a nuclear war. To adopt that kind of course in the nuclear age would be evidence only of the bankruptcy of our policy—or of a collective death-wish for the world.

To secure these ends, America's weapons are nonprovocative, carefully controlled, designed to deter, and capable of selective use. Our military forces are committed to peace and disciplined in self-restraint. Our diplomats are instructed to avoid unnecessary irritants and purely rhetorical hostility.

For we can seek a relaxation of tensions without relaxing our guard. And, for our part, we do not need to use threats to prove that we are resolute. We do not need to jam foreign broadcasts out of fear our faith will be eroded. We are unwilling to impose our system on any unwilling people—but we are willing and able to engage in peaceful competition with any people on earth.

Meanwhile, we seek to strengthen the United Nations, to help solve its financial problems, to make it a more effective instrument for peace, to develop it into a genuine world security system—a system capable of resolving disputes on the basis of law, of insuring the security of the large and the small, and of creating conditions under which arms can finally be abolished.

At the same time we seek to keep peace inside the non-Communist world, where many nations, all of them our friends, are divided over issues which weaken Western unity, which invite Communist intervention or which threaten to erupt into war. Our efforts in West New Guinea, in the Congo, in the Middle East, and in the Indian subcontinent, have been persistent and patient despite criticism from both sides. We have also tried to set an example for others—by seeking to adjust small but significant differences with our own closest neighbors in Mexico and in Canada.

Speaking of other nations, I wish to make one point clear. We are bound to many nations by alliances. Those alliances exist because our concern and theirs substantially overlap. Our commitment to defend Western Europe and West Berlin, for example, stands undiminished because of the identity of our vital interests. The United States will make no deal with the Soviet Union at the expense of other nations and other peoples, not merely because they are our partners, but also because their interests and ours converge.

Our interests converge, however, not only in defending the frontiers of freedom, but in pursuing the paths of peace. It is our hope—and the purpose of allied policies—to convince the Soviet Union that she, too, should let each nation choose its own future, so long as that choice does not interfere with the choices of others. The Communist drive to impose their political and economic system on others is the primary cause of world tension today. For there can be no doubt that, if all nations could refrain from interfering in the self-determination of others, the peace would be much more assured.

This will require a new effort to achieve world law—a new context for world discussions. It will require increased understanding between the Soviets and ourselves. And increased understanding will require increased contact and communication. One step in this direction is the proposed arrangement for a direct line between Moscow and Washington, to avoid on each side the dangerous delays, misunderstandings, and misreadings of the other's actions which might occur at a time of crisis.

We have also been talking in Geneva about other first-step measures of arms control, designed to limit the intensity of the arms race and to reduce the risks of accidental war. Our primary long-range interest in Geneva, however, is general and complete disarmament—designed to take place by stages, permitting parallel political developments to build the new institutions of peace which would take the place of arms. The pursuit of disarmament has been an effort of this Government since the

1920's. It has been urgently sought by the past three administrations. And however dim the prospects may be today, we intend to continue this effort—to continue it in order that all countries, including our own, can better grasp what the problems and possibilities of disarmament are.

The one major area of these negotiations where the end is in sight, yet where a fresh start is badly needed, is in a treaty to outlaw nuclear tests. The conclusion of such a treaty, so near and yet so far, would check the spiraling arms race in one of its most dangerous areas. It would place the nuclear powers in a position to deal more effectively with one of the greatest hazards which man faces in 1963, the further spread of nuclear arms. It would increase our security—it would decrease the prospects of war. Surely this goal is sufficiently important to require our steady pursuit, yielding neither to the temptation to give up the whole effort nor the temptation to give up our insistence on vital and responsible safeguards.

I am taking this opportunity, therefore, to announce two important decisions in this regard.

First: Chairman Khrushchev, Prime Minister Macmillan, and I have agreed that high-level discussions will shortly begin in Moscow looking toward early agreement on a comprehensive test ban treaty. Our hopes must be tempered with the caution of history—but with our hopes go the hopes of all mankind.

Second: To make clear our good faith and solemn convictions on the matter, I now declare that the United States does not propose to conduct nuclear tests in the atmosphere so long as other states do not do so. We will not be the first to resume. Such a declaration is no substitute for a formal binding treaty, but I hope it will help us achieve one. Nor would such a treaty be a substitute for disarmament, but I hope it will help us achieve it.

Finally, my fellow Americans, let us examine our attitude toward peace and freedom here at home. The quality and spirit of our own society must justify and support our efforts abroad. We must show it in the dedication of our own lives—as many of you who are graduating today will have a unique opportunity to do, by serving without pay in the Peace Corps abroad or in the proposed National Service Corps here at home.

But wherever we are, we must all, in our daily lives, live up to the age-old faith that peace and freedom walk together. In too many of our cities today, the peace is not secure because freedom is incomplete.

It is the responsibility of the executive branch at all levels of government—local, State, and National—to provide and protect that freedom for all of our citizens by all means within their authority. It is the responsibility of the legislative branch at all levels, wherever that authority is not now adequate, to make it adequate. And it is the responsibility of all citizens in all sections of this country to respect the rights of all others and to respect the law of the land.

All this is not unrelated to world peace. "When a man's ways please the Lord," the Scriptures tell us, "he maketh even his enemies to be at peace with him." And is not peace, in the last analysis, basically a matter of human rights—the right to live out our lives without fear of devastation—the right to breathe air as nature provided it—the right of future generations to a healthy existence?

While we proceed to safeguard our national interests, let us also safeguard human interests. And the elimination of war and arms is clearly in the interest of both. No treaty, however much it may be to the advantage of all, however tightly it may be worded, can provide absolute security against the risks of deception and evasion. But it can—if it is sufficiently effective in its enforcement and if it is sufficiently in the interests of its signers—offer far more security and far fewer risks than an unabated, uncontrolled, unpredictable arms race.

The United States, as the world knows, will never start a war. We do not want a war. We do not now expect a war. This generation of Americans has already had enough—more than enough—of war and hate and oppression. We shall be prepared if others wish it. We shall be alert to try to stop it. But we shall also do our part to build a world of peace where the weak are safe and the strong are just. We are not helpless before that task or hopeless of its success. Confident and unafraid, we labor on—not toward a strategy of annihilation but toward a strategy of peace.

A Selected Bibliography

Bailey, Thomas A., *Presidential Greatness*. New York: Appleton-Century-Crofts, 1966.

Binckley, Wilfred E., *President and Congress*, 3d ed. New York: Random House Inc., 1962.

Burns, James MacGregor, *Presidential Government*. Boston: Houghton Mifflin Company, 1966.

Cornwell, Elmer E., Jr., *Presidential Leadership of Public Opinion*. Bloomington, Ind.: Indiana University Press, 1965.

Corwin, Edward S., *The President: Office and Powers, 1787-1957*, 4th ed. New York: New York University Press, 1957.

Corwin, Edward S., and Louis W. Koenig. *The Presidency Today*. New York: Harper & Row, Publishers, 1956.

Fenno, Richard F., *The President's Cabinet*. Cambridge, Mass.: Harvard University Press, 1959.

Finer, Herman, *The Presidency: Crisis and Regeneration*. Chicago: University of Chicago Press, 1960.

Henry, Laurin L., *Presidential Transitions*. Washington, D.C.: The Brookings Institution, 1960.

Herring, E. Pendleton, *Presidential Leadership*. New York: Farrar, Straus & Giroux, Inc., 1940.

Hyman, Sidney, *The American President*. New York: Harper & Row, Publishers, 1954.

Kallenbach, Joseph E., *The American Chief Executive*. New York: Harper & Row, Publishers, 1966.

Koenig, Louis W., *The Chief Executive*. New York: Harcourt, Brace & World, Inc., 1964.

Laski, Harold J., *The American Presidency*. New York: Grosset & Dunlap, Inc., 1960.

Longaker, Richard P., *The Presidency and Individual Liberties*. Ithaca, N.Y.: Cornell University Press, 1961.

May, Ernest R., *The Ultimate Decision*. New York: George Braziller, Inc., 1960.

Neustadt, Richard E., *Presidential Power*. New York: John Wiley & Sons, Inc., 1960.

Rankin, Robert S., *et al., The Presidency in Transition.* Gainesville, Fla.: Kallman, 1949.

Rossiter, Clinton, *The American Presidency.* New York: Harcourt, Brace & World, Inc., 1960.

Sorensen, Theodore C., *Decision Making in the White House: The Olive Branch or the Arrows.* New York: Columbia University Press, 1963.

Tugwell, Rexford G., *Enlargement of the Presidency.* New York: Doubleday & Company, Inc., 1960.

Warren, Sidney, *The President As World Leader.* Philadelphia & New York: J. B. Lippincott Co., 1964.